W9-ATM-383

50 Hikes in Western Pennsylvania

50 *Hikes*

In Western Pennsylvania

Walks and Day Hikes from the
Laurel Highlands to Lake Erie

TOM THWAITES

Third Edition

Woodstock, Vermont

An Invitation to the Reader

Housing developments, logging, mining, fires—
these and other works of man and nature take
their toll on hiking trails. If you find that
conditions along any of these 50 hikes have
changed, please let the author and publisher
know so that they may correct future editions.
Address correspondence to:

Editor
Fifty Hikes™ Series
Backcountry Guides
P.O. Box 748
Woodstock, VT 05091

Library of Congress
Cataloging-in-Publication Data

Thwaites, Tom.
Fifty hikes in western Pennsylvania : walks and
day hikes from the Laurel Highlands to Lake Erie
/ Tom Thwaites ; photographs by the author.—
3rd ed.
    p. cm. – (50 hikes series)
Includes bibliographical references.
ISBN 0-88150-473-4 (pbk. : alk. paper)
1. Hiking—Pennsylvania Guidebooks.
2. Pennsylvania Guidebooks.
I. Title. II. Title: 50 hikes in western Pennsylvania. III. Series: Fifty hikes series.
GV199.42.P4T49   1999
917.4804'43–dc21   99–28303
                                        CIP

Text and cover design by Glenn Suokko
Cover photo by Robert Bossi
Interior photographs by Tom Thwaites
Original trail maps by Richard Widhu
New maps on pages 10, 26, 33, 57, 61, 76, 90,
93, 96, 103, 107, 115, 131, 135, 141, 165,
168, 183 by Mapping Specialists, Ltd.,
Madison, Wisconsin, © 2000 The Countryman
Press

© 1983, 1990, 2000 by Tom Thwaites

Third Edition

All rights reserved. No part of this book may be
reproduced in any form or by any electronic or
mechanical means, including information storage
and retrieval systems, without permission in
writing from the publisher, except by a reviewer,
who may quote brief passages.

Published by Backcountry Guides
A division of The Countryman Press
P.O. Box 748
Woodstock, VT 05091

Distributed by W.W. Norton & Company, Inc.
500 Fifth Avenue
New York, NY 10110

Printed in the United States of America
10 9 8 7 6 5 4

To my wife, Barbara

50 Hikes at a Glance

HIKE	REGION
1. James Wolfe Sculpture Trail	Laurel Highlands
2. Ferncliff Natural Area	Laurel Highlands
3. Meadow Run	Laurel Highlands
4. Grove Run Trail	Laurel Highlands
5. Wolf Rocks Trail	Laurel Highlands
6. Charles F. Lewis Natural Area	Laurel Highlands
7. Mt. Davis Natural Area	Laurel Highlands
8. Cucumber Falls	Laurel Highlands
9. Laurel Hill State Park	Laurel Highlands
10. Whitetail Trail	Laurel Highlands
11. Blue Hole Creek	Laurel Highlands
12. Mountain Streams Trail	Laurel Highlands
13. Roaring Run Natural Area	Laurel Highlands
14. Bear Run Nature Reserve	Laurel Highlands
15. Quebec Run Wild Area	Laurel Highlands
16. New Florence Game Lands	Laurel Highlands
17. Maple Summit to Ohiopyle	Laurel Highlands
18. Hearts Content Scenic Area	Allegheny National Forest
19. Anders Natural Area	Allegheny National Forest
20. Beaver Meadows	Allegheny National Forest
21. Browns Run	Allegheny National Forest
22. Tom's Run	Allegheny National Forest
23. Buzzard Swamp	Allegheny National Forest
24. Clear Creek State Park	Allegheny National Forest
25. Beartown Rocks	Allegheny National Forest

	DISTANCE (miles)	WILDFLOWERS	WATERFALLS	VIEWS	NOTES
	1.8			★	Inclined Plane; sculptures
	2.1		★		Ohiopyle Falls
	3.2		★		Cascades and slides
	4.2		★		Waterfalls
	4.5			★	Panoramic view
	5.0		★	★	Views, waterfalls, and wildlife
	5.8				Highest point in PA; mountain laurel and rhododendron
	5.9	★	★		Waterfalls; spring wildflowers; car shuttle required
	7.7				Old-growth hemlock; Laurel Hill Lake
	7.9			★	Views
	8.0				Mountain streams
	8.0				Mountain streams
	8.2	★			Mountain stream; spring wildflowers
	8.8	★		★	Mountain streams; backcountry campsites
	8.9				Wild area; mountain streams; backcountry campsites
	10.5				Laurel Highlands Trail; iron furnace
	11.3			★	Laurel Highlands Trail; car shuttle required
	1.1				Virgin timber; log display; wheelchair accessible in part
	2.0				Old-growth white pines
	3.6				Lake; shadbrush; evergreens; blueberries
	3.7				Evergreens; North Country Trail; car shuttle required
	4.0				Mountain stream; Tanbark Trail; logging railroad grades
	5.1				Ponds; birds
	5.2				Evergreen plantations; pileated woodpeckers
	5.9			★	View; black forest

50 Hikes at a Glance

HIKE	REGION
26. Cook Forest State Park	Allegheny National Forest
27. Minister Creek Trail	Allegheny National Forest
28. Brush Hollow Trail	Allegheny National Forest
29. Chapman State Park	Allegheny National Forest
30. Clarion–Little Toby Trail	Allegheny National Forest
31. Tracy Ridge Trail	Allegheny National Forest
32. Hickory Creek Trail	Allegheny National Forest
33. Wolf Creek Narrows Natural Area	Pittsburgh and the Southwest
34. Jennings Environmental Education Center	Pittsburgh and the Southwest
35. Wildflower Reserve	Pittsburgh and the Southwest
36. Beechwood Nature Trails	Pittsburgh and the Southwest
37. Harrison Hills Park	Pittsburgh and the Southwest
38. McConnells Mill State Park	Pittsburgh and the Southwest
39. Glacier Ridge Trail	Pittsburgh and the Southwest
40. Hidden River Bridge	Pittsburgh and the Southwest
41. Ryerson Station State Park	Pittsburgh and the Southwest
42. Slippery Rock Gorge Trail	Pittsburgh and the Southwest
43. Enlow Fork	Pittsburgh and the Southwest
44. Raccoon Creek State Park	Pittsburgh and the Southwest
45. Presque Isle State Park	Erie and the North
46. Oil Creek State Park	Erie and the North
47. Erie Extension Canal Towpath	Erie and the North
48. Petroleum Center	Erie and the North
49. Allegheny Gorge	Erie and the North
50. M. K. Goddard State Park	Erie and the North

DISTANCE (miles)	WILDFLOWERS	WATERFALLS	VIEWS	NOTES
6.3			★	Virgin timber; lookout tower
6.3			★	View; cliffs; mountain stream
6.3			★	Mountain streams; cross-country skiing
7.5	★		★	Views; spring wildflowers
7.5				Ghost towns; mountain streams
10.3				North Country Trail; backpacking possible
11.6				Old logging camp; backpacking possible
1.5	★			Spring wildflowers
2.2	★			Prairie wildflowers; massasauga rattlesnakes
2.4	★			Wildflowers
2.5				A pleasant walk
2.5			★	Views, Rachel Carson Trail
3.2	★	★		Gorge; waterfalls; rapids; wildflowers; old mill; covered bridge
4.7			★	North Country National Scenic Trail; car shuttle required
4.6				Glacier Ridge Trail; Hidden River Bridge
5.3				Ryerson Lake
6.1	★			Wildflowers; wild gorge; big trees; car shuttle required
6.6	★			Wildflowers and birds
8.3				Small lake; pleasant walk in the woods
3.9				Lake Erie; lighthouse
5.3				Oil Creek Gorge; backcountry shelters
6.0				Pymatuning Swamp; waterfowl
7.1		★		Waterfall; ghost town
7.3			★	Old iron furnace; view; mountain stream
12.8				Lake Wilhelm

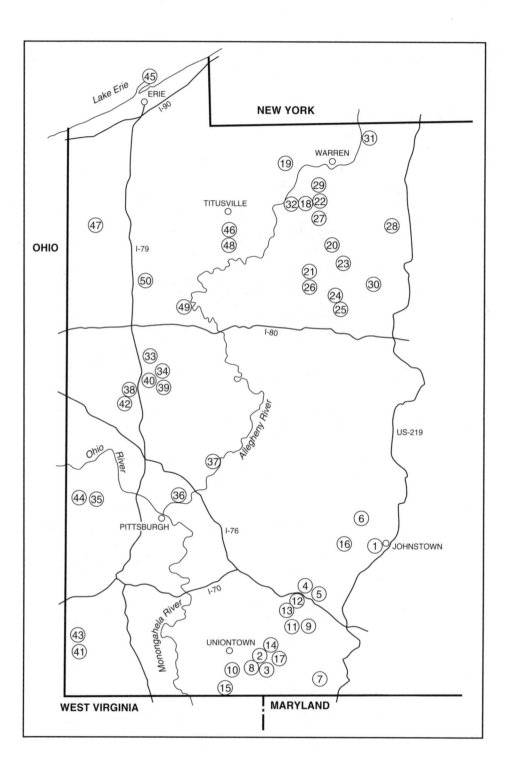

CONTENTS

III. PITTSBURGH AND THE SOUTHWEST

IV. ERIE AND THE NORTH

Acknowledgments

This book could not have been written without the help of many hikers living in western Pennsylvania. Among those who suggested hikes were Mary Ann and Steve McGuire, Glenn Oster, Bill Dzombak, Ray Gerard, Ruth and Norm Samuelson, Paul Wiegman, Jerry Bosiljevac, Bob Peppel, Hugh Downing, Dave Maxwell, Janeal Hedman, Sylvia Grisez, Bernice Beck, Jim Ritchie, Rhonda Hoover, Dick Pratt, and Mark Eckler. I thank them as well as others who didn't give their names or whose names I didn't write down. I am particularly grateful to my wife, Barbara, who served as hiking companion, driver, typist, editor, and critic.

Introduction

Walking may be the best exercise, but it can be difficult to find a place where you can walk in comfort and safety. The newer parts of towns are often devoid of sidewalks. It is dangerous to walk on busy roads, and doing so may attract the attention of the police. Children are required to ride the bus to school, and corner stores have fled to distant malls. Strip malls may physically bar you from walking along them. Only the most fortunate live close enough to walk to work (this was an unappreciated feature of the company town). In the past, highway bridges routinely incorporated a walkway, but today even intersections are posted NO PEDESTRIAN CROSSING.

We have organized walking out of our lives. You have to drive somewhere before you can walk, but private lands are often posted NO TRESPASSING, and many public lands are overrun with conflicting uses that can make walking unpleasant or even dangerous. This book will guide you to places where foot travel is not just tolerated but encouraged.

What's the difference between a walker and a hiker? The principal difference is a pack. If you get too warm, you can shed a layer and put it in your pack. If you get thirsty, you can take out your canteen and have a drink. If you get hungry, you can take out your lunch or snack. If it starts to rain, you can take out your raingear.

Hiking is not only good aerobic exercise for young and old, but it brings us closer to nature and our roots in the natural world. Hiking reminds us that food does not come from the supermarket, wood does not come from the lumberyard, and water does not come from the faucet. Hikers share the delights and dilemmas of those who cannot live without things that are natural, wild, and free. In hiking, no one keeps score, everybody wins, and you are the most valuable player.

Public Lands, Public Lands, and Public Lands

Hikers are generally restricted to public lands, and these are relatively scarce in western Pennsylvania. Foremost is Allegheny National Forest (ANF), located in the northern part of the state along the New York State border and administered by the U.S. Department of Agriculture for both recreation and timber. For some people national is the only kind of public land that matters, and at roughly 200,000 hectares (494,000 acres), ANF is the largest single tract of public land in Pennsylvania west of US 219.

Next are some 100,000 hectares (247,000 acres) of state game lands widely distributed across the western part of Pennsylvania. One is even found in Allegheny County just outside Pittsburgh. The Pennsylvania Game Commission is primarily supported by user fees in the form of licenses and other taxes paid by hunters, but the acquisition of game lands is also supported from general tax revenues and contributions from corporations and individuals. Game lands are administered primarily for hunting, but timber is also harvested. There are comparatively few trails on game lands, but gated maintenance roads can be used instead.

Both state parks and forests are administered by the Department of Conservation and Natural Resources, though their missions are different. Parks are people oriented and feature picnic areas, campgrounds, and swimming areas. Forests are managed for timber and water production, and their recreation is hiking, hunting, and fishing. The three state forests west of US 219 (Forbes, Clear Creek, and Cornplanter) range in size from modest to tiny. Some state parks like Raccoon, Moraine, Laurel Hill, and Ohiopyle are large, but most are of modest size. State parks are usually well developed with hiking trails.

Over the years the Western Pennsylvania Conservancy has purchased land that is now incorporated into state parks, forests, and game lands. Many of the best hiking areas in western Pennsylvania—including large parts of Ohiopyle, McConnells Mill, Moraine, Oil Creek, and Laurel Ridge State Parks as well as Forbes State Forest and Jennings Environmental Center—were purchased by the Western Pennsylvania Conservancy and transferred to public ownership. Sometimes it seems that a hiker would not legally be able to step off a road in western Pennsylvania were it not for the conservancy.

Geography

Western Pennsylvania is a plateau cut through by many river valleys. Before the Ice Ages most of these rivers, including the Youghiogheny and the Allegheny, flowed northwest into the Saint Lawrence River, where Lake Erie is today. Glacier after glacier profoundly altered the northwestern part of the state, dotting the area with lakes, swamps, and bogs and changing the course of rivers well beyond the reach of the ice. Some rivers had to reverse their flow. The Allegheny and Ohio Rivers of today contain sections where the flow has been reversed.

Along the hikes in this book you will see evidence of the energy and mineral resources of the commonwealth. Coal is only one energy resource in Penn's Woods. In 1859 the world's first oil well was drilled near Titusville. More than a century later oil and gas wells are still being drilled.

Pennsylvania's location is a happy one with respect to insects. It is just far enough south to escape black flies and just far enough north to avoid most ticks—at least the big brown dog ticks. But there are gnats that, while a distant second to black flies, try harder. Mosquitoes are abundant in the swampy areas. Deer flies can be a real nuisance as they try to carve off a steak.

On Hiking

Emotional as well as physical benefits are gained from hiking. John Muir wrote: "Climb the mountains and get their good tidings. Nature's peace will flow into you as sunshine flows into trees. The winds will blow their own freshness into you, and the storms their energy, while cares will drop off like autumn leaves."

Aldo Leopold wrote: "Never did we plan the morrow, for we had learned that in the wilderness some new and irresistible distraction is sure to turn up each day before breakfast."

M. K. Gandhi said: "Of all the vows I took, those about traveling on foot have been the most beneficial."

George W. Sears (1821–1890) was Pennsylvania's pioneer conservationist and outdoor writer. "Nessmuk," as Sears was called, put it this way: "We do not go to the ... woods to rough it, we go to smooth it. We get it rough enough ... in towns and cities."

It's true! Whenever pressures and problems drive me to the woods, the miracle works again. A few hours of hiking, a view of the countryside, and I can feel my problems drop away or shrink into perspective. I am freshly astonished.

About This Book

Detailed instructions are given here for fifty hikes on public lands or private lands where hiking is permitted.

All the hikes in this book were measured with a Rolatape two-meter measuring wheel. The distance given for each hike is how far you will walk to complete the hike as described. Where hikes can be shortened, instructions are included.

Hiking times are determined by SOAP/WP (standard old-aged pace with pacemaker). Those who have just taken up hiking may find their times exceed mine. Young hikers in good condition will have no trouble shortening them. But keep in mind that hiking is not competitive; it is the quality of the experience that counts.

The rise listed for each hike is the total amount of climbing obtained by adding together all the ups in an up-and-down hike. In some car-shuttle hikes—such as Maple Summit to Ohiopyle—the rise would be greatly increased if the hike were done in the opposite direction. In all cases the rise has been determined from the USGS 7 ½' topographic maps.

There are 19 short or introductory hikes in this book. They range up to 8 kilometers (5 miles) long and up to three hours' hiking time. Novice hikers should try one or more of these short hikes before moving up to day hikes. Twenty-six hikes range from 8 kilometers (5 miles) to 16 kilometers (10 miles) and are classed as day hikes. Some of these could be turned into 2-day backpacks.

Finally, there are five "bootbuster" hikes ranging from 16 kilometers (10 miles) to 20.6 kilometers (12.8 miles). These are challenges for the most seasoned hikers. Again, some of them could be turned into backpacks.

Pennsylvania roads range from interstates down to doubtful dirt, but some of the most confusing are simply designated as state routes. These roads are generally paved but marked only with obscure little black-and-white signs at intersections and sometimes elsewhere. On top in small characters the signs say, for example, SR 1234. This is the important information, and the directions to many trailheads are given in terms of SR numbers. Below it in larger characters is a number that you can ignore.

Maps are listed in each description. United States Geological Survey (USGS) maps are always listed but usually don't show the actual trails. State park maps are better for trails, but do not show contours. The best trail maps are those prepared by the organization responsible for trail maintenance. Copies of the "Pennsylvania Recreation Guide and Highway Map," which lists state parks and their facilities and activities, are available from the Office of Public Information of the Department of Conservation and Environmental Resources and at most state park offices. For information on where to order maps, see the list of addresses at the end of the introduction.

The fifty hikes are grouped into four geographic areas. Thirty-two hikes are concentrated in the Laurel Highlands and Allegheny National Forest areas. The remainder are in the Pittsburgh or Lake Erie areas, which are divided by I-80.

Equipment and Clothing

Hiking clothes should be comfortable. They don't have to be new or fashionable or expensive. In summer, when the primary task is keeping cool, hiking shorts and short-sleeved shirts are appropriate. You're going to sweat a lot more come summer. The only equipment required is a day pack for carrying your canteen, insect repellent, and rain gear if the weather looks threatening. Don't try to cram these items into your pockets.

Your best bet for rain gear are items made of Gore-Tex, but if these are too expensive, the good old waterproof nylon poncho still works.

Most hikers carry their water in leakproof plastic Nalgene bottles. If you leave some space for expansion, you can freeze the water in a plastic bottle in the freezer overnight and thereby provide yourself with a supply of ice water on the trail. The only advantage of a metal canteen is that you can put it directly on a stove in winter to thaw the ice trying to form inside.

In fall and spring the demands on clothing escalate. Temperatures may vary from near freezing in the morning to pleasantly warm on a sunny afternoon. Also, the weather can turn hypothermic with little or no warning. These are the seasons when you appreciate wool and polypropylene clothing. You may need one of the larger day packs to carry the layers you will shed as the day warms up in addition to the items already mentioned.

Winter conditions are highly variable across western Pennsylvania. Snow depths may reach a meter or more in the Alleghenies and on Laurel Ridge, while other places may be bare. Deep snow requires snowshoes or cross-country skis; trying to hike without them leads quickly to exhaustion. Hypothermia is even more of a threat in winter. It can rain in winter, too. Yet there is as much beauty in the woods in this season as in the others.

Backpacking requires a lot more equipment than day hiking. You will need a sleeping bag, a backpack, and some kind of shelter. Since you'll spend about one third of your time in the sleeping bag, it's important to get one that's really comfortable. Mummy bags are much warmer than traditional rectangular bags, but some people find mummy bags too confining. A bewildering variety of designs and materials is available, including some compromises between rectangular and mummy bags. For Appalachia's temperate rain forest, synthetic fillings such as Polarguard and Hollofill are your best bets. They are slightly heavier than down but are cheaper and will keep you warm even if they get wet. Line the stuff sack with a plastic bag to make sure your sleeping bag stays dry.

A good backpack is basically a collection of pockets of various sizes. The internal frame packs so popular today are designed to aid your balance for cross-country skiing and mountain climbing. For general-purpose backpacking, the external frame pack is still best. Backpacks should be fitted to your height. If a store wants to sell you a backpack without trying it on, take your business elsewhere. A padded hip belt allows you to transfer 50 to 90 percent of the pack's weight directly to your hips, bypassing all those fragile discs in your back.

Adirondack-type shelters are available only on the Laurel Highlands and Gerard Trails, where they must be reserved in advance. These shelters have an open front, a good roof, and a fireplace. Elsewhere in western Pennsylvania, you will have to carry your own shelter. A waterproof nylon tarp is the lightest and cheapest solution. However, when bugs are bad, you'll need a tent with good ventilation. Again, a variety of designs is available, and the best advice is to rent before you buy.

An item of equipment that can greatly reduce your impact on the landscape is a backpacking stove. It leaves no pile of charcoal at your campsite and poses a minimal fire hazard. Many types of fuels are available, and you should try several before investing in your own. When buying hiking and backpacking equipment, beware of large retail chains. Seek out an outdoor store where the clerks know what they are selling.

Footwear

The most important and specialized part of a hiker's equipment is footwear. Shoes or boots for hiking must have good arch support and should also protect your feet from impacts with rocks, roots, sticks, and logs. Ideally, your footwear should also keep your feet dry in rain, snow, or wet brush. Besides being cold and uncomfortable, wet feet develop blisters far faster than dry ones.

Leather hiking boots with lug soles are almost ideal. Lug soles look like a flexible waffle iron. These boots are available at outing stores. Cheaper alternatives involve a variety of compromises. Be sure to get boots of full-grain leather with as few seams as possible. With good care, they should carry you along the trail for years to come.

The worst thing that can happen to leather shoes or boots is to get them soaked. But if you do, drying must be done slowly at room temperature. Even a few such soakings will greatly reduce the life of a leather boot. Purchase boots large enough so that you can wear at least two pairs of socks—a thin inner sock of polypropylene and a thick mostly wool outer sock—without cramping your feet. Leather boots must be waterproofed, usually with some form of Nikwax which will have to be periodically reapplied.

Safety in the Woods

Just a few years ago the woods were very safe. Once you got a few healthy trees between you and the nearest road, the chances of your being severely injured dropped dramatically. The mountain bike has changed this. Now the dangers of the road can follow you down the trail and run you down, over, and off in some remote locations. I have tried to devise hikes on trails where mountain bikes are prohibited, but this hasn't always been possible. Enforcement of such prohibitions is sadly lacking. On rail trails bikes are a minimal hazard because these trails are wide, flat, and relatively straight. It's on narrow, steep mountain trails that mountain bikes pose a threat to hikers.

Autumn, with its crisp, cool weather, bright blue skies, and brilliantly colored leaves, is an enchanting time to hike Penn's Woods, but almost every fall day is hunting season for some animal or bird. Hunters wear orange. So should you. Orange hats and vests are sold at most outing-goods stores. Unless you're a hunter, stay out of the woods in both bear season (3 days starting the Monday before Thanksgiving) and deer season (2½ weeks starting the Monday after Thanksgiving).

Don't worry about snakes. They are rare, generally shy, and belong on the endangered species list in Pennsylvania. Besides, they are big enough to see. Just don't pick them up. Most snake bites occur on hands and arms.

The biggest threats to your health are microbial. First is giardia and other microbes found in streams, springs, and unprotected water sources. Fill your canteen before you leave home, or get your drinking water from tested supplies. On a backpack trip you will have to use untested sources. Pump the water through a submicron filter such as

MSR, PUR, or First Need to remove giardia cysts and bacteria.

Another threat is Lyme disease, a potentially fatal disease that is transmitted to humans by a tiny creature often no larger than the period at the end of this sentence. Symptoms of Lyme disease include skin rash, flu, stiff neck, chills and fever, extreme fatigue, swollen glands, sore throat, severe headaches, body aches, joint and bone pains. If Lyme disease is untreated, arthritic, neurological, and cardiac symptoms can also develop. One of the difficulties in diagnosing Lyme disease is that it resembles so many other diseases. Blood and urine tests for Lyme disease are useful but not completely reliable.

Precautions include wearing long pants tucked into your socks and long-sleeved shirts. (Unfortunately in summer this is insufferably hot.) Apply insect repellent containing DEET to your pantlegs, socks, and shoes.

If you do wear shorts, you'll have to apply DEET on your exposed skin. Be forewarned that DEET is absorbed through the skin and is suspected of causing epileptic-type seizures in children. When hiking, keep to the middle of the trail, and don't lie down or sit in tall grass or other vegetation. When you get home, inspect yourself for ticks and then shower to sluice off any unattached ticks. Clothing should be thoroughly washed and then dried at high temperature.

Lyme disease can be treated at all stages with antibiotics; as with other diseases there is a premium on early treatment. If you think you may have been exposed, call the American Lyme Disease Foundation at 1-800-876-LYME for the name of a physician in your area who specializes in treating Lyme disease.

Two vaccines for Lyme disease have been developed. LYMErix, developed by Smith Kline Beecham, tested out to be 79 percent effective at preventing Lyme disease. A series of three injections spread out over a year are required, so the vaccine is only 50 percent effective the first year. Booster shots will probably be required but have not yet been approved. An unusually guarded FDA approval was given to LYMErix. ImuLyme, developed by Pasteur Merieux Connaught of Swiftwater, PA, is claimed to be 92 percent effective and FDA approval is expected in 1999.

Stinging insects—hornets, wasps and yellow jackets—are another hazard in Penn's Woods. Yellow jackets nest underground, even in the middle of trails. You usually don't know you have stepped into a nest until you feel the first fiery sting. Then all you can do is run through some brush, swiping and swatting, to escape the vengeful horde.

Cold, wet weather presents the hazard of hypothermia. If you get soaked at any time when the temperature is below 10 degrees Celsius (50 degrees Fahrenheit), you are in trouble. Garments of wool, pile, Polarguard, Hollofill, Thinsulate, etc., are your best defense against hypothermia. Even in the initial stages, before uncontrollable shivering sets in, your judgment and perception are insidiously impaired. Be alert for signs of hypothermia in your companions. Slurred or incoherent speech, stumbling, falling, and violent shivering are all signs of hypothermia. Treatment consists of getting the victim out of cold, wet clothing and into dry clothes. Warm the victim by getting him or her into a shelter and/or a sleeping bag. Warm, not hot, liquids may be given, but alcoholic beverages will only make things worse.

Another threat from the weather is lightning. Don't stand under a tall tree or in an open field when lightning is around. For once, a car is about the safest place to be.

Lastly, beware of any wild animal that doesn't flee at your approach. An animal that acts strangely must be suspected of having rabies. Should you be bitten by *any* animal, including a bat, make every effort to kill it so that its brain can be tested by the veterinary diagnostic laboratory in Harrisburg. If the animal escapes, you will have to undergo the entire series of shots for rabies.

Respect for the Land and Its Inhabitants

Once you step off a road, your environmental impact increases dramatically. It used to be that man felt threatened by nature. But the numbers of our species have reversed this rule. Now it's the land and its wild inhabitants that are vulnerable. Carry out litter in your pack or pockets; don't leave it to degrade the landscape. Some of our litter—bottles and aluminum cans—is of geologic permanence. Be careful with fire. Forest fires kill woods and wildlife. Never leave a campfire unattended: Make sure it is dead out before you move on. Try to build a campfire only where one has been built before, and use only dead and down wood for fuel. Don't smoke in the woods. Refrain from collecting wild plants or injuring live trees or shrubs.

Although hikers' use of the land constitutes the lightest of human impacts, even it can be overdone. Avoid overused hiking and camping areas. And stay on designated trails so as to not impact the ecosystem.

You can help improve hiking and backpacking in Penn's Woods. The Appalachian Trail was built largely by volunteers and is maintained exclusively by them. The North Country Trail, from New York to North Dakota, is being built by volunteers. Join one or more of the organizations listed below that are involved in building and maintaining hiking trails. A few people with hand tools can work miracles. Physically and emotionally, the rewards of trail work are as real as they are little known.

Hiking Organizations

Keystone Trails Association
P.O. Box 251
Cogan Station, PA 17728
keyhike@sunlink.net
Updates to the hikes in this book will be given in the "Hiker Alert" column of the Keystone Trails Association Newsletter.

Western Pennsylvania Conservancy
209 Fourth Avenue
Pittsburgh, PA 15222
412-288-2774
pwiegman@paconserve.org

Sierra Club, Allegheny Group
c/o Peter Wray
110 Royal Oak Ave.
Pittsburgh, PA 15235
pjwray@telerama.com

Hosteling International, Pittsburgh
830 East Warrington Ave.
Pittsburgh, PA 15210
412-431-4910
ayh@trfn.clpgh.org

Allegheny Outdoor Club
c/o Bill Massa
109A E. Wayne St.
Warren, PA 16365
masa@allegany.com

North Country Trail Association—
 Pennsylvania
P. O. Box 2968
Butler, PA 16003-2968
Bob_Tait@nauticom.net

Other Books

Pennsylvania Hiking Trails, 12th ed.
Keystone Trails Association, 1998.
*Hiker's Guide to the Laurel Highlands
Trail,* 4th ed. Sierra Club–Allegheny
Group, 1992.
Allegheny National Forest Hiking Guide,
3rd ed. Sierra Club–Allegheny Group,
(1990).
Baker Trail Guide. Hosteling
International–Pittsburgh, 1997.
*Best Hikes with Children in
Pennsylvania.* Sally Trepanowski, The
Mountaineers, 1996.
Hiking Pennsylvania, Rhonda and George
Ostertag, Falcon, 1998.

Maps and Where to Get Them
United States Geological Survey Maps:
Distribution Branch
US Geological Survey
Box 25286 Federal Center, Bldg. 41
Denver, CO 80225
($4.00 per map)

State park maps:
From individual state park offices or:
Bureau of State Parks
P.O. Box 8551
Harrisburg, PA 17105-8551
Phone: 1-800-63 PARKS

Public use maps for state forests:
From individual state forest offices or:
Department of Conservation and
Environmental Resources
P. O. Box 8552

Harrisburg, PA 17105-8552

State game lands recreation maps:
Pennsylvania Game Commission
Dept. AR, 2001 Elmerton Ave.
Harrisburg, PA 17110
(50¢ per map)

Web sites:
Keystone Trails Association: http://www.
kta–hike.org; Allegheny National Forest:
http://www.penn.com/~anf

U.S. Forest Service maps:
Allegheny National Forest
Box 847
Warren, PA 16356
814-723-5150
($4.00 charge for Allegheny National
Forest map)

I

Laurel Highlands

Cucumber Falls

1

James Wolfe Sculpture Trail

Distance: 3.0 km (1.8 miles)

Time: 1½ hours

Rise: 10 meters (40 feet)

Highlights: View; sculptures

Maps: USGS 7½' Johnstown

Johnstown is located at the confluence of Stony Creek and Little Conemaugh River, just before they cut their way through Laurel Hill to the west. This location brought the Pennsylvania Canal and then the railroad through Johnstown, but on May 31, 1889 it also brought disaster. But the Great Flood of '89 was not the only flood or only disaster to strike Johnstown.

This is an urban hike in the middle of Johnstown. By taking the Inclined Plane to the top of Yoder Hill, you eliminate virtually all climbing. The hillside is covered with large trees, and bird calls compete with traffic noises from PA 56 on the other side of Stony Creek.

The trailhead is the base station at the foot of the Inclined Plane. Coming from the west on PA 56 it's a right-hand turn up the ramp. From the east, provision is made for a left-hand turn. There is space for several cars to park on the ramp, and additional parking can be had along PA 56 just east of the bridge over the highway. If both of these places are full there is additional parking in the downtown area, including a parking garage.

You only have to buy a one-way ticket for the Inclined Plane since you will be walking back. At the top of Yoder Hill, take a good look out over Johnstown because the trail is heavily wooded. Then turn left and walk 150 meters (500 feet) along the street, passing some picnic tables. There is a post sign at the top of the hiking trail and also a sign saying NO BIKES. The first switchback is the only bad one. A large tree has fallen here and not been removed. The switchback has

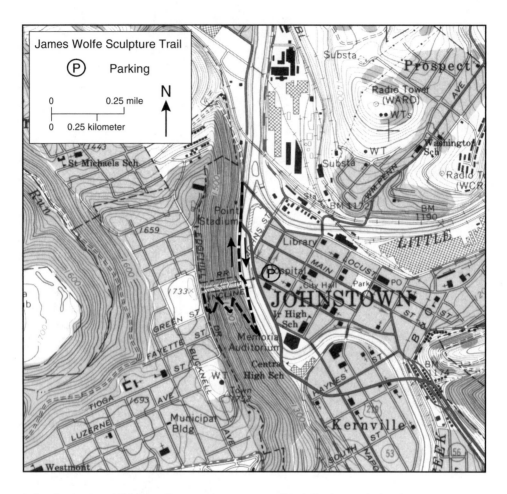

to be shortcut, and this is a slippery process even in dry weather. For this one corner it would be worth wearing your hiking boots.

The trail then leads downhill, passing a walled spring. The trail is not marked and crosses a number of other grades, but it's still easy to follow. There are post signs at a couple of confusing turns. In spring, mayapples, jack-in-the-pulpits, and red trilliums bloom along the trail. Many wet areas are bridged. At 0.5 meters (0.3 mile) turn left on an old road. Then turn right on the trail. Climb up a few steps at 0.8 meters (0.5 mile) to reach a bridge. Trees growing on the hillside are tulip, locust, and red maple.

Turn left on an old road at 1.3 km (0.8 mile). You are now almost at the bottom of the hill, and Stony Creek can be seen below. At 2.1 km (1.3 miles) pass under the Inclined Plane, and climb a slope to the James Wolfe Sculpture Trail. Wolfe was the artist who designed these creations, but the sculptures were actually built by 136 local steelworkers from the Bar, Rod, and Wire Division of Bethlehem Steel. They were made for the 100th anniversary of the Great Flood to show the spirit of Johnstown.

Fred and Ginger

Most of the figures are to your left, including one called Fred and Ginger. Hint: Fred has a top hat.

Continue out this grade to the site of another disaster. This is the mouth of a coal mine in which 112 men were killed on July 10, 1902. Johnstown has had more than its fair share.

There is a last sculpture at 2.5 km (1.5 miles). Through the trees you can see the seven-arch stone railroad bridge. Much of the wreckage of Johnstown piled up here in the Great Flood—and caught fire. Those trapped in their houses were burned alive. Over 2200 bodies were found, but another 900 were simply missing.

Turn here and retrace your steps to the incline. Ring the bell and exit from the trail system. At the far side of the bridge over Stony Creek note the high-water mark of May 3, 1889.

You may also want to visit the Johnstown Flood Museum. Take the pedestrian crosswalk over PA 56, walk a couple of blocks on Main Street, and turn left on Walnut. A couple more blocks brings you to the museum in an old library building at 304 Washington Street.

To visit the site of the South Fork Dam (whose collapse created the Great Flood), drive east on PA 56 for 5 miles. Then take US 219 north for 5 miles, exit on PA 869 east, and follow signs to the visitor center on the far side of the former lake.

2

Ferncliff Natural Area

Distance: 3.3 km (2.1 miles)

Time: 1½ hours

Rise: 60 meters (200 feet)

Highlight: Ohiopyle Falls

Maps: USGS 7½' Ohiopyle, Fort Necessity; state park map

Ferncliff is a peninsula surrounded on three sides by the Youghiogheny River, (pronounced: YAHK-ah-gainy). The river's name, like many others in Pennsylvania, is a white man's corruption of an Indian name. In this case the name is supposed to mean "stream flowing in a roundabout course." It is a magical area that reminds me of Point Lobos on the California coast. Perhaps it's the roar of the rapids and falls that is reminiscent of the surf. But it's also the sense of remoteness and isolation. Nearby Ohiopyle village and the rest of the state park seem completely cut off by the violence of the river. Around the Ferncliff Peninsula the Youghiogheny drops 30 meters (100 feet) in just 1.5 km (1 mile), producing Ohiopyle Falls and half a dozen rapids. Another point of resemblance to Point Lobos is the poison ivy that keeps you on the trails.

As with several other natural areas and reserves, Ferncliff Natural Area was originally acquired and operated by the Western Pennsylvania Conservancy.

The peninsula was formed by the gradual retreat of Ohiopyle Falls. At one time or another, the Youghiogheny may have flowed over the entire peninsula. Potholes, such as you see at the brink of the falls, are also found above today's river level. The Youghiogheny River flows from the mountains to the south and brings with it seeds of southern plants. Thus Ferncliff is the northern outpost for many southern plants. Among these is the buffalo nut, a parasitic shrub that grows on the roots of mountain laurel. The Buffalo Nut Trail at

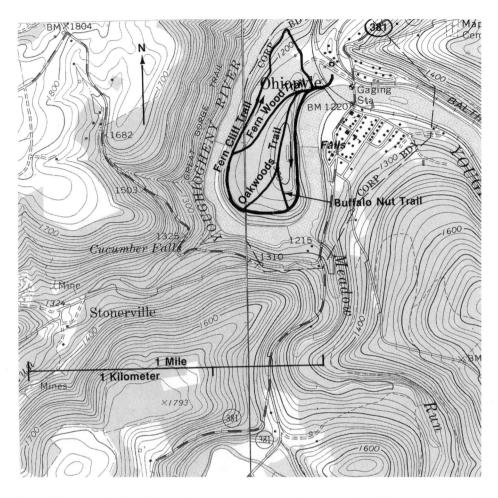

Ferncliff is named after this shrub.

Walking shoes are fine for this short hike. The trailhead can be reached only from PA 381. Turn west just north of the bridge over the Yough and before you reach the two tracks of the Baltimore & Ohio Railroad. Bear left at the sign into one of the parking lots. Follow the signs to the trailhead. The Ferncliff Trail is a self-guiding nature trail and is marked with low-impact black blazes. These blazes are easier to follow than you might think. The trail takes you under the old Western Maryland Railroad bridge to a trail junction and marker noting that Ferncliff

was declared a National Natural Landmark in 1973. Follow the Ferncliff Trail as it bears left to emerge at the water's edge. There is a life ring and line, but the line is a dreadful tangle. Near 0.3 km (0.2 mile) look for a fossil tree fern in the bedrock. It stretches almost entirely across the trail and is probably a lepidodendron, or scale tree. Soon you see poison ivy edging the trail mostly on the right. Note driftwood logs lodged high above the normal level of the river. The shore here is bordered with thick jungles of rhododendron. When you reach the brink of the falls, the trail is forced out

---

onto the ledges. Then turn back into a tunnel through the rhododendron. Near 0.6 km (0.4 mile) turn left for an overlook of Ohiopyle Falls. The falls are formed by the resistant Pottsville sandstone.

The overlook is from the brink of a cliff and has no guardrails, so watch your step. Perhaps it was from this very spot that George Washington viewed the falls in 1754 while trying to find a way to move men and supplies for the attack on Fort Dusquesne. He may have thought that the reports of the waterfall had been exaggerated—waterfalls never lose much in the reporting process. But George was convinced and gave up the idea of water travel on the Yough. To the right you can see the put-in place for today's travel on the lower Yough by kayak and raft.

Back on the trail you climb to the top of the cliff, tunneling through the rhododendron between large hemlocks and white pines. At 0.9 km (0.6 mile) you reach another overlook, where the Buffalo Nut Trail comes in from the right. A picturesque white pine stands at the edge of the cliff. You can hear but not see Entrance Rapids from this point.

Oakwoods Trail comes in from the right at 1.1 km (0.7 mile), and shortly at a large white pine there is a side trail that leads to the edge of the river. Back on the Ferncliff Trail, ignore the next side trail, since it doesn't lead to any good view. At 1.9 km (1.2 miles) keep left as the Fernwood Trail diverges to the right. The trail returns to the cliff side, and you can hear more rapids below. An unsigned trail goes right at 2.4 km (1.5 miles), and soon you turn left to an overlook that provides a good view of the rapids.

At 2.7 km (1.7 miles) bear right, and the trail will take you through a stand of hemlocks set about with boulders. From here you can hear the roar of yet another set of rapids—probably Railroad Rapids. Next, you turn right to take the trail back across the base of Ferncliff Peninsula. Along the way you cross a small meadow and then bear left at the trail junction to return to your car.

For an unusual hike, follow the Takeout Trail loop to the foot of Railroad Rapids. Many river runners portage and put in again just below the falls. From the takeout you can see the Western Maryland Railroad bridge across the Yough. Note how much higher this bridge is than the one just scarcely 600 meters (2,000 feet) away at the village of Ohiopyle. That's how much the river has fallen in its trip around the Ferncliff Natural Area.

Additional hiking opportunities at Ohiopyle include Meadow Run Trail (Hike 3) and Cucumber Falls (Hike 8).

3

Meadow Run

Distance: 5.1 km (3.2 miles)

Time: 2 hours

Rise: 135 meters (445 feet)

Highlight: Cascades and slides

Maps: USGS 7½' Ohiopyle; state park map

This short but delightful trail is located in Ohiopyle State Park on PA 381. The side streams that flow into the Youghiogheny have to cut through the same hard sandstone that forms Ohiopyle Falls, so these streams have their own waterfalls and cascades. Ohiopyle is said to mean "white frothy water," an apparent reference to the falls of the Youghiogheny.

The trailhead is a large parking area on SR 2011, just 0.1 mile from PA 381. Ohiopyle State Park can be reached from PA 711 at Normalville and US 40 at Farmington by PA 386. Good walking shoes should be fine for this hike. Bicycles are prohibited on the Meadow Run Trails.

Of the three trails from the parking lot, take the one farthest to the right. It has a sign for Meadow Run and is marked with yellow paint blazes. The trail climbs up the side of a hill, passing rhododendron, goldenrod, and crab apple trees. It then enters older woods, where tulip trees are abundant, and descends on an old road. Bear right at an intersection with another old road.

A critical turn is reached at 1.0 km (0.6 mile). Bear left off the old road and descend on stone steps through cliffs. (Just when you really need a blaze there isn't a one to be seen.) The trail then follows the base of the cliffs, passing under overhangs before turning and reaching Meadow Run. At 1.3 km (0.8 mile) there's a side trail to the cascades and at 1.4 km (0.9 mile), another. These cascades over ledges of bare rock seem to be what the park map designates as a waterfall.

The cascades at Meadow Run

Continue downstream, climbing to the top of a rise and then descending through hemlocks and rhododendrons. Flat Rock is reached by a side trail at 2.3 km (1.4 miles). Just beyond, the Loop Return Trail bears left to the parking lot, offering a chance to truncate the hike.

Deep Hole is reached just a few steps beyond this junction. Next, the trail passes along the base of the hill before climbing it on steps.

At 3.0 km (1.9 miles) there's a critical junction. There is no sign, but a yellow-blazed trail turns left. You'll need to find this junction on your way back from the slides. Continue downstream, and soon you see PA 381 farther up the slope.

At 3.4 km (2.1 miles) there is a critical turn to the right, and the trail descends through a break in the cliffs. If you miss this turn, a herd path leads out to the highway.

Follow the blazes carefully. Next, turn sharp left, and soon you are back next to Meadow Run. The trail continues along ledges above the run but at one point crosses a bridge with a distinct list to starboard. Use caution because the antiskid surface has all but vanished.

You have reached the slides. These are natural water slides, and at some risk you can slide down them on your backside. The wet rock is very slippery.

When you're finished admiring—or enjoying—the slides, retrace your steps to the junction of yellow-blazed trails. This time keep right, and climb through a gap in an old stone wall to the parking lot and your car.

Additional hiking at Ohiopyle can be found at Ferncliff Natural Area, on the far side of the Yough (Hike 2), and at Cucumber Falls (Hike 8) and Boughman Trail on this side.

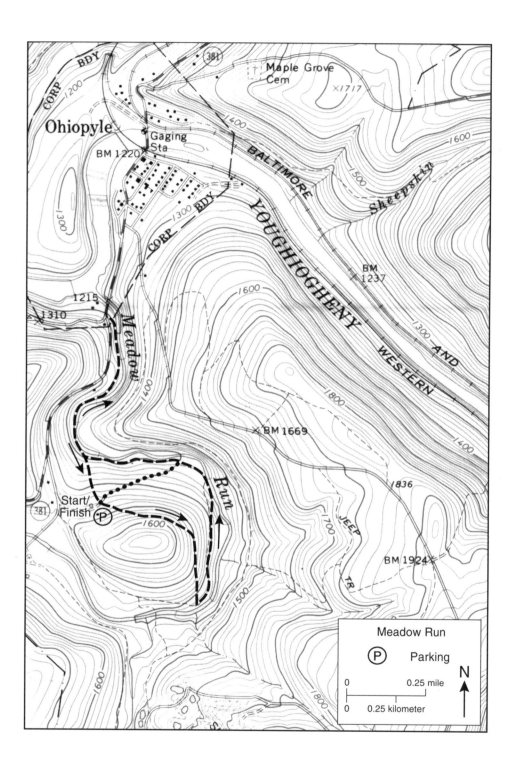

Ohiopyle

Maple Grove Cem

BM 1220

Gaging Sta

BM 1237

BM 1669

Start/Finish

Meadow Run

YOUGHIOGHENY

BALTIMORE

Sheepskin

WESTERN AND

BM 1924

JEEP TR

Meadow Run

Ⓟ Parking

N

0   0.25 mile

0   0.25 kilometer

4

Grove Run Trail

Distance: 6.7 km (4.2 miles)

Time: 2¾ hours

Rise: 260 meters (850 feet)

Highlight: Waterfalls

Maps: USGS 7½' Ligonier; state park map

Linn Run State Park is a small state park on the western side of Laurel Hill surrounded by Forbes State Forest. These lands had been clear-cut by the time the state purchased them from Byers and Allen Lumber Company in 1909; the Pittsburgh, Westmoreland & Somerset Railroad, built for the logging, had started many fires on the cutover land; and the deer had all been killed. So there was criticism of the state for spending money on such wasteland. Today we are the beneficiaries of the state's foresight. Deer were reintroduced from Michigan and New York. The forest reclaimed the brier patches and fern fields. The Linn Run Road has almost obliterated the Pittsburgh, Westmoreland & Somerset Railroad tracks. In the 1930s the Civilian Conservation Corps built many of the structures in the park. More recently, these have been rebuilt by the Youth Conservation Corps and Pennsylvania Conservation Corps.

The Youth Conservation Corps also built an attractive hiking trail up Grove Run, over the height-of-land to the east and down Boot Hollow Run. The trailhead is located at Grove Run Picnic Area, which is on the Linn Run Road 3.0 miles southeast of the small village of Rector (on PA 381). Ordinary walking shoes should be fine for this short hike, but you will appreciate your boots when sidehilling Boot Hollow. In places the ground cover is catbrier, so long pants are in order.

Drive through the picnic area, which is equipped with a piped spring and rest

Grove Run Trail

right of the trail; then at 2.0 km (1.2 miles) you turn left across the remainder of the stream, and continue climbing across the hillside. The trail switchbacks up the steep slope. The abundance of greenbrier, a vinelike thorny plant, discourages you from shortcutting the switchbacks. Despite its thorns, greenbrier—a catbrier—is food for deer, bear, grouse, turkey, and smaller animals. On these drier slopes, chestnut oak is the most common tree.

There's a trail register at the end of one switchback. Take the time to sign in. You still have some climbing ahead, so this is a good place for a breather.

After another switchback, you reach the top of the hill at 2.9 km (1.8 miles) and cross the Quarry Trail, which is part of the Laurel Highlands snowmobile trail system. Just beyond, keep left where another blue-blazed trail diverges to the right and ultimately leads to Fish Run. Soon you cross a watercourse and start down into Boot Hollow. The trail cuts along the side of the steep slope, where there may be some leaves-off views across Linn Run Valley, although in summer the green curtain is opaque.

Next, you cross the snowmobile trail again and at 5.4 km (3.3 miles) you bear left on new trail cut by volunteers in 1989. This trail, which is also blue-blazed, avoids the Linn Run Road by traversing the hillside above Linn Run. The new trail soon passes above a spring, and for a bit it picks up an old footway, but mostly it's all brand new. Descend and cross Grove Run as best you can. In high water you could go downstream and use the road bridge. The trail continues to the piped spring in Grove Run Picnic Area.

Two short hikes are found farther up Linn Run. On the north side, the Darr Trail and Brant Trail make a short loop, using part of the old Rector Edie Road. On the south

rooms, and park in the small area at the far end. The blue-blazed Grove Run Trail begins here. Pass around the gate, and then step across the outlet from a spring to the right of the trail. The trail starts out easily along an old logging road, but at 0.6 km (0.4 mile) you bear right and climb up the side of the valley. Trees along this section of the trail are tulip, red oak, and red maple.

Farther along, the stream—which often flows underground in the lower parts of the valley—returns to the surface. After you cross Grove Run on a bridge just below a small pool, swing left, and climb up the valley of a tributary. Next, you pass a waterfall that can be seen and heard in the narrow valley below you. Trees along this stretch are basswood, sugar maple, beech, and striped maple *(Acer pennsylvanicum)*. Soon you cross the spot where most of the tributary comes down across mossy ledges to the

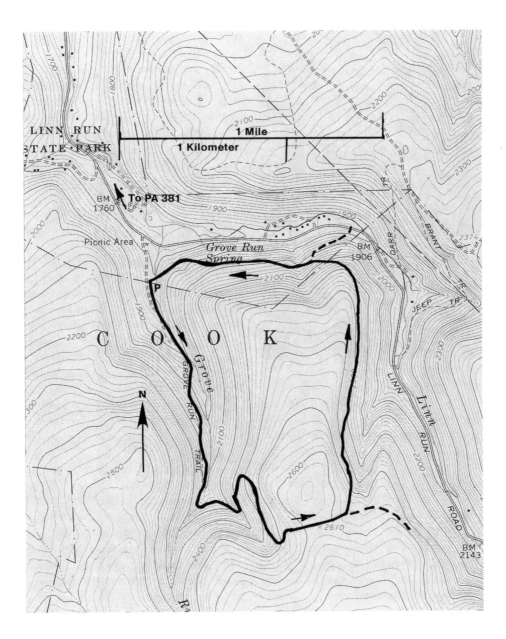

side, the Fish Run Trail leads to the remains of the Pittsburgh, Westmoreland & Somerset Railroad. You can also make a loop by returning along Fish Run. The park has obtained a grant to build a trail along Linn Run itself.

5

Wolf Rocks Trail

Distance: 7.3 km (4.5 miles)

Time: 2½ hours

Rise: 60 meters (200 feet)

Highlight: Panoramic view

Maps: USGS 7½' Ligonier, Bakersville; Forbes State Forest Public Use map; Linn Run State Park map.

Natural overlooks are rare in Pennsylvania. Since no part of the state approaches timberline in elevation, rocky cliffs provide the only views. Such cliffs are uncommon, and trees below frequently grow tall enough to shut off the view. Although Laurel Hill is broad and flat on top, further reducing the chances for a natural overlook, this hike surmounts all these obstacles and provides a 180-degree panorama above Linn Run.

The hike starts from Laurel Summit State Park, which is also the access point for Spruce Flats Bog. The origin of this depression on top of Laurel Ridge is obscure. The bog had progressed to a mature stand of hemlock (which is frequently confused with spruce) when it was logged in 1908. It turned out that the transpiration of the trees had been responsible for removing the water from this undrained depression. With the trees gone, the water table rose, and the bog was reformed. All efforts at reforestation have failed; to become forest again, the bog must repeat the natural succession.

Laurel Summit State Park is 5.8 miles south of US 30 on the Laurel Summit road. Turn at the sign for Laurel Mountain Ski Resort. The park can also be reached from PA 381 at Rector via the Linn Run road. Water, a picnic shelter, and tables, as well as pit toilets, are available at the park.

The roads in the park appear to have been spurs on the Pittsburgh, Westmoreland & Somerset Railroad, which was built across Laurel Ridge at the turn of the 19th century to serve the Byers and Allen sawmill at Ligonier. Chartering the railroad separately from the sawmill established it as a "common carrier"

The view from Wolf Rocks

and permitted it to condemn rights-of-way when needed. Although the PW&S eventually reached Somerset, using part of the right-of-way built for the South Penn Railroad (Vanderbilt's Folly), its name can only have sprung from 19th-century optimism, for it never had the remotest hope of reaching Pittsburgh. The South Penn right-of-way was owned at that time by the Baltimore & Ohio, which did not grant the PW&S permission, so building the PW&S without permission was an act of corporate chutzpah. The grades across Laurel Hill were stiff, but rod locomotives were able to negotiate them. Geared shay locomotives were used only on logging spurs where grades hit 12 percent.

The Wolf Rocks Trail is fairly flat. A loop has been added for cross-country skiing. Ordinary walking shoes should be fine for this hike, but the trail is rocky, and you will appreciate boots. Catbriers along the way say to wear long pants.

From the parking lot bear left to the corner where the red blazes begin. (The blue ones have faded into oblivion.) At 0.3 km (0.2 mile)

you cross a pipeline swath. The trail continues along the fringes of the Spruce Flats Bog, where rhododendron thrives. The bridge over a tiny stream has been replaced by a culvert and at 1.0 km (0.6 mile) you reach a signed trail junction. (Spruce Flats Trail goes right here.) Turn left on Wolf Rocks Loop, which is also red blazed.

Turn right at 2.5 km (1.5 miles) and then cross some more culverts at 2.9 km (1.8 miles). Despite high use on Wolf Rocks Loop, parts of the trail are covered with moss. Farther on, this ski trail has been bulldozed up a particularly rough section. At 3.4 km (2.1 miles) turn left on the old Wolf Rocks Trail at a signed junction. Next, pass the blazed but unsigned Bobcat Trail, and arrive at Wolf Rocks at 3.9 km (2.4 miles). You can see down Linn Run Valley and across to Chestnut Ridge in the west. You can also see up Fish Run Valley, just across from you, and up to the top of Laurel Hill itself. Rhododendron and mountain ash grow around Wolf Rocks, adding to its appeal.

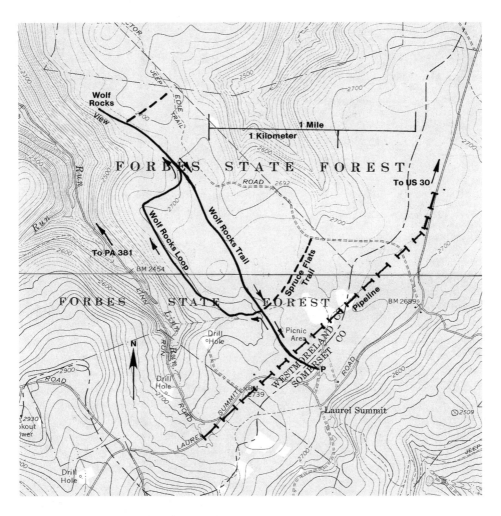

To return, follow the old Wolf Rocks Trail. Go straight ahead at 4.3 km (2.7 miles), and then pass an unmarked trail to the left at 5.4 km (3.3 miles). At 6.3 km (3.9 miles), continue ahead at the other end of the Wolf Rocks Loop, and retrace your steps to the picnic area.

There is a nearby hike at Linn Run State Park (Hike 4). The Laurel Highlands Hiking Trail runs to the east of the summit and can be reached by the Hickory Flats Road. Most other trails on this part of Laurel Hill, including the old Rector Edie Road, have been turned over to mountain bikes.

6

Charles F. Lewis Natural Area

Distance: 8.1 km (5.0 miles)

Time: 3½ hours

Rise: 410 meters (1340 feet)

Highlights: Views; waterfalls

Maps: USGS 7½' Vintondale; Natural Area map

The Charles F. Lewis Natural Area is a small portion of Gallitzin State Forest, located on Laurel Ridge northeast of the Conemaugh Gorge. Dr. Charles Fletcher Lewis, for whom the area is named, was a newspaperman, conservationist, and first president of the Western Pennsylvania Conservancy.

The natural area, although only 155 hectares (383 acres), is suitably wild and rugged. It's reported to have an abundance of rattlesnakes, and one buzzed at me on my first hike. Reptiles and amphibians are protected within the natural area. I also encountered a pileated woodpecker, and at one point in the trail I was confronted by a large black object. Then it moved and snorted, and I realized it was a bear. At the sound of her snorts, her cubs (two at least) shot up a basswood tree, and I fumbled in my pack for a telephoto lens. But Mama snorted again, the cubs quickly returned to the ground, and by the time I had my camera ready, they had all vanished into the woods.

The Charles F. Lewis Natural Area is located on PA 403 in the Conemaugh Gorge, 3.5 miles south of US 22 and 5.9 miles from the PA 56 junction in Johnstown. There is plenty of parking space. The trails are steep, rocky and wet, so hiking boots are in order.

To start the hike, head across the open area and pass through the arch at the start of the yellow-blazed Clark Run Trail. At 140 meters (460 feet) bear right up the steps. You will return over Clark Run to your left. At 275 meters (900 feet) you can see the best of the waterfalls on the run. Trees growing in this part of the valley are basswood, beech, and yellow birch.

Conemaugh Gorge

The steepest part of the climb is over by the time you reach a charcoal flat at 1.2 km (0.7 mile). There are many more of these charcoal flats on Laurel Ridge. They supplied charcoal to the iron industry in the 19th century. (Two charcoal iron furnaces can be seen in the New Florence game lands in Hike 16.)

A trail junction is reached at 1.3 km (0.8 mile). The yellow-blazed Clarks Run Trail turns left on a woods road. Beware: The orange blazes of the Rager Mountain Trail are also present! To pick up the Rager Mountain Trail, jog right 10 meters (about 30 feet) on the old road, and head up the flight of steps. The Rager Mountain Trail climbs the ridgeline between Clark Run and Conemaugh Gorge. At 2.4 km (1.5 miles) you cross a 500-kilovolt power line swath that provides views of Conemaugh Gorge and Laurel Ridge.

Continuing on the Rager Mountain Trail, the ridge becomes very narrow, and you pass an outcrop of cross-bedded sandstone. The ridge then broadens out as you approach the upper portions of Rager Mountain. Cross an old road at 3.3 km (2.1 miles). Just beyond is a charcoal flat.

Cross Rager Mountain Road at 3.6 km (2.2 miles) and recross the power line swath at 4.1 km (2.5 miles). There is a view down the Conemaugh River and generally over the C. F. Lewis Natural Area. You jog right on an old woods road at 4.4 km (2.7 miles) and at 4.8 km (3.0 miles) you jog right again on a snowmobile trail. The white-blazed state forest boundary is reached at 5.3 km (3.3 miles) and the trail parallels it for about 300 meters (1,000 feet). Along this stretch a mysterious (not shown on any map) red-blazed trail takes off to the left. Cross a deeply eroded old road.

At 6.5 km (4.0 miles) you reach the Clark Run Trail, which comes in from the left on an old road. To the right you can see a gate blocking the road at the edge of state forest land. Follow the Clark Run Trail across the road. This trail becomes rough and rocky as it cuts across the side of the valley and is an

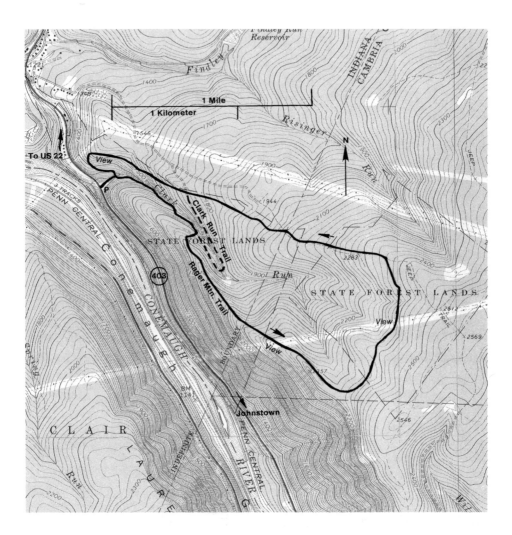

ideal place to meet rattlesnakes, so watch your step. There are cliffs to the right, and you pass through clumps of rhododendron and mountain laurel. At 7.1 km (4.4 miles) you top out along the state forest boundary. A view rock to the left is reached at 7.5 km (4.7 miles). It provides a vista across Clark Run Valley and up Conemaugh Gorge.

Back on the trail, you soon turn left and descend steeply at times through very rocky terrain. At 7.8 km (4.8 miles) turn left on a road that's the old route of the paved highway. The original highway bridge over Clark Run is gone, so you must bear left off the old highway and proceed upstream. Cross the stream as best you can, and bear right on the trail you came in on. You are soon back at your car.

Additional hiking opportunities in this area are on the other side of Conemaugh Gorge and Hike 16, farther south near New Florence.

7

Mt. Davis Natural Area

Distance: 9.4 km (5.8 miles)

Time: 3¾ hours

Rise: 225 meters (740 feet)

Highlights: Highest point in Pennsylvania; mountain laurel and rhododendron

Maps: USGS 7½' Markleton; public use map—Forbes State Forest

Of all the states in the Appalachian Mountains, Pennsylvania has the lowest high point. At 979 meters (3,211 feet), it is a serious disappointment to peak baggers. Yet Mt. Davis has character. Unlike the highest point of one midwestern state, it is not in the middle of a cornfield. The trees are stunted, and even on a sunny day it has an alpine feel. But the weather is frequently foul; even in midsummer there can be fog so thick that you can't see the ground from the top of the 50-foot observation tower.

Mt. Davis Natural Area is 235 hectares (580 acres) of state forest surrounding the high point on what was formerly called Negro Mountain. The peak is named for an early settler and former owner of the area, while legend has it that the mountain is named for a black man who was killed there when he and his companions were set upon either by Indians or a wounded bear or other wild animal. The incident may have taken place to the south, in Maryland, where the mountain reaches a higher elevation.

This is a circuit hike using the Mt. Davis picnic area on SR 2004 as a trailhead. The picnic area is 9.2 miles from Meyersdale, which in turn is about 22 miles south of Somerset on US 219. In Meyersdale, turn west on Broadway Street (SR 2004) and follow the occasional signs for Mt. Davis. A bit west of town you can see Mt. Davis ahead of you, particularly the large microwave relay tower that is just across the road from the picnic area. Coming from the west on US 40, turn north on PA 523 for 1.5 miles, and then turn east in Listonburg. Pass

A leafy trail in the Mt. Davis Natural Area

High Point and Deer Valley Lakes to reach the picnic area and trailhead at 17.1 km (10.7 miles) from Listonburg. The high point of Mt. Davis itself could be used as an alternative trailhead, which would shorten the hike by 0.6 km (0.4 mile). Outhouses and a pump for drinking water are available at the picnic area. The picnic area and much of the land covered on the Tub Mill Run Trail were added to Forbes State Forest after the USGS map was printed. Considering the rocks and stream crossings, you'll want your boots for this hike.

To start your hike, head uphill to the top of the picnic area, and then turn left on the High Point Trail. All trails at Mt. Davis have been blazed with blue-plastic markers nailed to trees. At 0.3 km (0.2 mile) turn left on the blue-blazed Tub Mill Run Trail. This junction is signed, and the markers are easy to follow. Jog left across Shelter Rock

Road at 0.9 km (0.6 mile) and proceed on the same trail. You continue to descend gently through banks of rhododendron and mountain laurel. The trail emerges at the edge of a pipeline swath that follows the eastern boundary of state forest land. Here I found the markers had been removed by vandals but the nails were left in the trees and were almost as easy to follow as the original markers. At 2.7 km (1.7 miles) you reach the edge of a small cliff set about with mountain laurel and rhododendron. Soon you cross a nameless tributary of Tub Mill Run and continue through the forest to 4.1 km (2.6 miles) where the trail parallels Tub Mill Run itself, which jumps from rock to rock under the rhododendrons and hemlocks. When the water is even moderately high, this is a delightful stream. Turn right for the Timberslide Trail, and cross Tub Mill Run at 4.6 km (2.9 miles).

Proceed to a junction with the Timber-slide Trail at the edge of a clear-cut dating from the mid '80s. Turn right, and start the climb up to Mt. Davis. At 5.5 km (3.4 miles) turn right on the Shelter Rock Road, which is closed to vehicles. Soon you pass Wildcat Spring a few paces to the right of the road. The water comes up through the sand so fast that it looks as if it were boiling. Next, you cross a bridge over Tub Mill Run—not nearly so exciting as your last crossing—and at 6.1 km (3.8 miles) at the top of a rise turn left on the Shelter Rock Trail. This trail is very straight, and a good deal of work has been done on the footway. Cross Tub Mill Run for the last time, and then pass a shelter rock to your left. At 6.6 km (4.1 miles) you reach the top of the hill. The trail takes you through a forest of stunted trees: black gum, pitch pine, oak, aspen, sassafras, and maple. It's not just the poor soil on the Pottsville sandstone but also the many ice storms and the generally inclement weather that keep

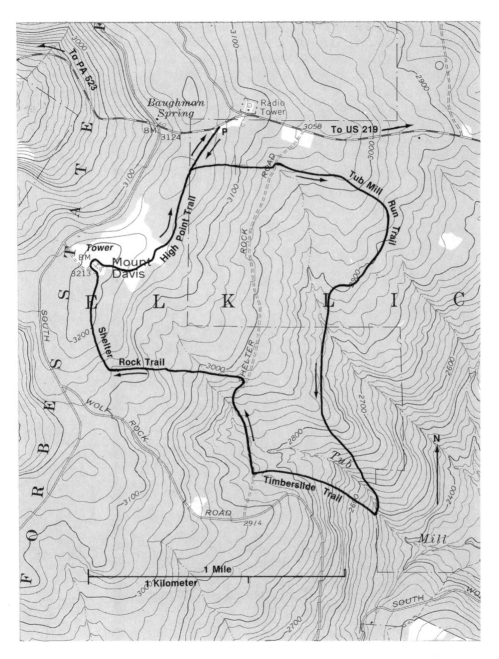

these trees so small. Pass through a section burned by a forest fire in 1993.

At 7.7 km (4.8 miles) the Mt. Davis Trail diverges to the right, providing a very short loop on top of Mt. Davis. Next you turn left and then right on the paved road to reach the base of the observation tower. If weather permits, climb the tower for com-

---

manding views in all directions. The vista from the tower includes stone circles to the north. These are formed when frost heaves elevate an area of soft soil, and over the years the rocks gradually slide down the sides. The ridge is so flat that points to the north and south actually appear higher than Mt. Davis. Careful surveying shows them to be lower, but it is a convincing optical illusion.

Continue to the exhibits, and cross the paved road to pick up the High Point Trail. The sign says PICNIC AREA 1 MILE. The Mt. Davis Trail soon comes from your right, and next you are back under larger trees. At 9.0 km (5.6 miles) you pass the junction with the Tub Mill Run Trail, and it's a short distance to the parking lot and your car.

Additional hiking opportunities are found south of the Mt. Davis Natural Area on the Livengood, Wolf Rock, and Laurel Run Trails, totaling over 6 kilometers (3.7 miles).

8

Cucumber Falls

Distance: 9.5 km (5.9 miles)

Time: 3½ hours

Rise: 135 meters (440 feet)

Highlights: Waterfalls; spring wildflowers

Maps: USGS 7½' South Connellsville, Mill Run, Fort Necessity, Ohiopyle; state park map

A tram road is a railroad that uses geared locomotives. Geared locomotives were developed for the 19th-century logging industry. Coal mining also involved heavy loads and steep grades, problems frequently solved with a tram railroad even into the first decades of the 20th century. This hike uses the grade of one such old railroad, now part of the Great Gorge Trail along Cucumber Run and the Youghiogheny River.

This hike requires a short car shuttle. Drive west on SR 2019 for 1.5 miles from PA 381 in Ohiopyle State Park. Continue ahead at the junction at the top of the hill for 1.6 miles more to a small parking lot on Jonathan Run, and leave one car here. Then drive back 2.7 miles to the Cucumber Falls parking area.

(Mountain bikes are now permitted on the lower portion of Jonathan Run Trail. They could be avoided in part by continuing along the Youghiogheny River Trail for a couple hundred yards beyond Jonathan Run Trail and following the Kentuck Trail up to Old Mitchell Place. The total distance would be much the same as the regular version of this hike, but the rise would be increased, and you would have to spot a car at Old Mitchell Place.)

The bridgeless crossing of Cucumber Run near the start of this hike can be avoided by crossing the bridge above Cucumber Falls and turning right on the Great Gorge Trail at the far side. Numerous wet spots and rocks make hiking boots better for this hike. However, with a little care, good walking shoes should do.

Dutchman's breeches along the Great Gorge Trail

To start, descend the steps on the north side of the road. At the first level you get the best view of the falls of the Cucumber. Continue down the switchbacks to the Yough and a junction with Meadow Run Trail. Turn left, and hunt for a spot where Cucumber Run is funneled between two large rocks. Here you can jump across. Keep left, pick up the yellow blazes, and follow the Meadow Run Trail as it climbs away from the Yough and ends at the Great Gorge Trail.

Turn right on this old tram road and follow it past one of the old coal mines. At 1.6 km (1.0 mile) you have to get off the railroad grade to cross a ravine. The bridge is long gone. The best displays of spring wildflowers are found along the Great Gorge Trail. Look for both red and white trilliums, Dutchman's breeches, and trout lilies. Somewhere beyond here the railroad ended, but a road continued to more mines farther along the gorge. At 2.2 km (1.4 miles) bear right to the old Western Maryland Railroad grade (Youghiogheny River Trail), and turn left. Then turn left again on the white-blazed Beech Trail, while Great Gorge Trail climbs the hill to the campground. Continue on the Beech Trail. At 2.6 km (1.6 miles) you come to another old coal mine, then at 3.4 km (2.1 miles) a rock overhang—a good place to wait out a shower.

At 4.2 km (2.6 miles), where the Beech Trail turns uphill through a break in the rhododendron-crowned cliffs, turn right, and descend steeply to the Western Maryland Railroad grade. Turn left on the grade, and look out for bicycles. With the completion of the bike trail upstream from Ohiopyle, bicycle usage at Ohiopyle State Park rose to equal the white-water usage. With the completion of this downstream bike trail, white-water usage will drop to second place. Despite all the trails in the park, hiking will be a distant third.

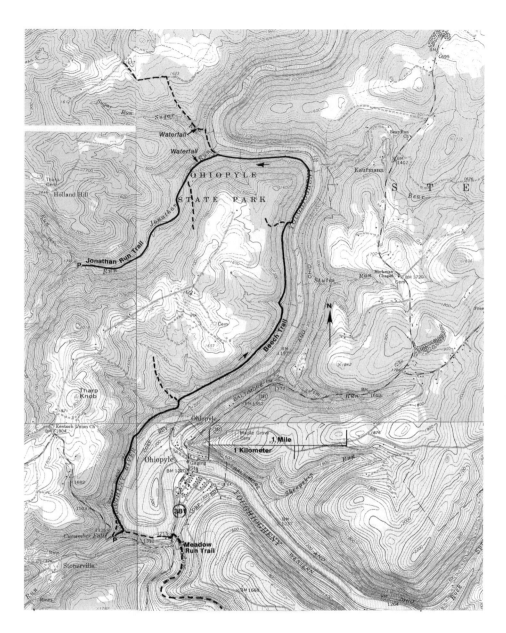

At 4.9 km (3.0 miles) you pass a small post that bears the letters *NN,* which stand for No Name Rapids. If a river runner is injured, help would be summoned by radio. The emergency vehicles would follow the Western Maryland Railroad grade to the rapids where the accident occurred. Since you usually can't see the river from the railroad grade, these posts tell the drivers where to stop.

Next the grade passes cliffs on the inside of a bend. Dimples and Swimmers

Rapids (DS) is passed at 6.0 km (3.7 miles) and Bottle of Wine (BW) at 6.5 km (4.0 miles). At 7.0 km (4.3 miles) turn left on the blue-blazed Kentuck Trail. If you miss this turn, the Western Maryland grade crosses a high fill above Jonathan Run. Back on the Kentuck Trail, bear right at 7.2 km (4.5 miles) for the best view of Jonathan Run Falls.

Continue ahead on the blue-blazed Jonathan Run Trail at 7.6 km (4.7 miles) where the Kentuck Trail turns uphill. Cross Jonathan Run on footbridges at 7.7 km (4.8 miles) and again at 8.1 km (5.0 miles).

Continuing up Jonathan Run you pass a clearing at 8.4 km (5.2 miles) with an old apple tree. Just beyond, climb the bank and follow a relocation to avoid further crossings of Jonathan Run. At 8.9 km (5.5 miles) turn sharply left, and follow another relocation to avoid a water damaged section of the old grade. After rejoining the old grade, continue upstream to the parking lot for Jonathan Run Trail.

Other hikes at Ohiopyle State Park are described in Hikes 2 (Ferncliff Natural Area), 3 (Meadow Run), and 17 (Maple Summit to Ohiopyle).

9

Laurel Hill State Park

Distance: 12.4 km (7.7 miles)

Time: 4¾ hours

Rise: 230 meters (760 feet)

Highlights: Old-growth hemlock; Laurel Hill Lake

Maps: USGS 7½' Bakersville, Seven Springs, Rockwood; state park map

Laurel Hill State Park, in Somerset County, ranks as one of the larger parks in western Pennsylvania, being almost 1,600 hectares (4,000 acres). Back in the 1930s, Laurel Hill was one of five federal demonstration parks in Pennsylvania. The others were Raccoon, Blue Knob, Hickory Run, and French Creek. After World War II these parks were transferred to the commonwealth, with the stipulation that they continue to be used for recreation. Two of the nine group camps at Laurel Hill were once Civilian Conservation Corps (CCC) camps. Try not to confuse Laurel Hill State Park (which is in Laurel Hill Creek valley) with Laurel Ridge State Park (which contains Laurel Highlands Hiking Trail) or with Laurel Mountain State Park (which is a downhill-ski area north of the turnpike).

Laurel Hill State Park can be reached from PA 31 just east of Bakersville by traveling south on SR 3037 for 1.7 miles to the eastern park entrance. The park can also be reached from PA 281 at New Centerville by driving west on SR 3029 for about 4.0 miles to the southern park entrance, just beyond the Trenthouse Inn B&B and Country Store. This hike starts from the large beach parking area, which is on the main park road connecting these two entrances, 0.7 mile from the south entrance and 2.8 miles from the east entrance. Stream crossings, rocks, and wet spots suggest boots for this hike.

Begin the hike by heading north along the park road. At the first road junction bear left on the road to Group Camp 8, which appears to be an old CCC camp, and go around the vehicle gate. At the far end of the group camp, continue straight ahead

Jones Mill Run Dam

into the woods on a snowmobile trail marked with orange diamonds, avoiding the road to the left. The ridge trail comes up from the right at 0.8 km (0.5 mile). Pass a water tank, and soon a trail comes in from the left. At 1.2 km (0.7 mile) bear right on the Pump House Trail, and descend gently to Jones Mill Run. Cross the run at 1.7 km (1.1 miles) on a snowmobile bridge, and immediately turn left on the Tram Road Trail. This is the route of a logging railroad, operated by the United Lumber Company, that hauled logs to a sawmill at Humbert, near the confluence of Laurel Hill Creek and the Casselman River.

Next, you come to a crossing of Jones Mill Run. If the water is high, you can avoid this crossing by bearing right because the Tram Road Trail soon returns to this side. Farther upstream there's another crossing that can also be avoided the same way since the Tram Road Trail recrosses the run just below the small dam.

The pond behind the dam is a popular spot with fishermen. Avoid the trail that the fishermen have worn along the edge of the pond. Instead, keep left on the Pump House Trail that comes in from the right. There have been some name changes from the old park map. A new park map that will more closely resemble the trail signs is expected in the near future. At 3.7 km (2.3 miles) cross the aqueduct, and immediately turn left on the unsigned Martz Trail.

At 4.0 km (2.5 miles) the Martz Trail meets the Koring Trail, which forms the border between Laurel Hill State Park and Forbes State Forest. Turn right on the Koring Trail, and ignore a road that soon diverges to the left. At 4.4 km (2.7 miles) turn right on the Bobcat Trail. This junction is signed, and the Koring Trail has reverted to the Beltz Road.

The Bobcat Trail is unblazed but much easier to follow than it used to be. At 5.0 km (3.1 miles) you cross Buck Run. Shortly

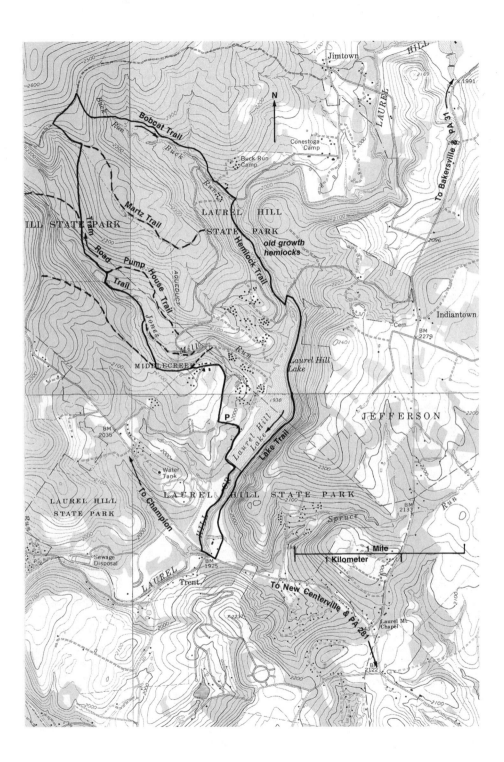

beyond the crossing there's a spring to the right of the trail. Farther on the trail parallels Buck Run, eventually crossing several tributaries. At 6.3 km (3.9 miles) turn left on Buck Run Road, and pass the Cub Scouts' Buck Run Camp. Note that bicycles are prohibited on Bobcat Trail.

Turn right at 6.6 km (4.1 miles) on the yellow-blazed Hemlock Trail, cross Buck Run, and turn left at a fork in the trail. The 4 acres of virgin hemlock are found at 6.9 km (4.3 miles). As usual with small patches of old-growth trees in Penn's Woods, the manner of their survival is not known. If a logger cut his neighbor's timber, he had to pay triple damages. So unless he had complete confidence in his surveyor, he was better off leaving uncut any small tracts of doubtful ownership. Perhaps these 4 acres are another monument to poor surveying. Turn sharp left at a sign for Hemlock Interpretive Trail, and follow the yellow blazes among the big trees next to Laurel Hill Creek.

Continue along the Interpretive Trail. Post 6 denotes that hemlock is the official state tree of Pennsylvania and that eastern hemlocks may live to nearly 1,000 years. Post 5 asks us to look at the stumps of trees cut long ago. They last longer than stumps of trees cut today because they are so much higher, due to being cut with a two-man crosscut rather than a chain saw. Laurel Hill Creek is acknowledged at post 4. Post 3 points out pioneer plants such as yellow birch that take over after the forest is disrupted by fire or logging. Post 2 draws our attention to runs darkened by tannic acid resulting from the decay of hemlock needles, and finally post 1 points out the excellent growing conditions in the bottoms along a stream.

The trail continues along a secluded section of Laurel Hill Creek. At 7.9 km (4.9 miles) turn left on the paved park road, cross

the bridge over Laurel Hill Creek, and then turn right on the Lake Trail. This is your last chance to shorten this hike by walking back along the park road. An old trailside shelter soon appears on the slope above the lake. This shelter was built of chestnut logs by the CCC before World War II. The roof is in bad shape, and it no longer provides any effective shelter. A bit down the trail is a piped spring. Camping is not permitted here.

The Lake Trail continues along the steep east side of Laurel Hill Lake. Sometimes it follows almost at the water's edge but often climbs far up the slope. At 9.9 km (6.2 miles) you reach the spillway, but there is no bridge across the creek here. Farther along avoid a trail that bears left into a larch plantation. The Lake Trail enters a meadow and then crosses a floating bridge over Spruce Run. When the water level rises, the bridge floats up, and then it settles back into place when the water drops. The trail skirts the edge of private land to emerge on the paved road SR 3029 at 10.9 km (6.8 miles). Turn right past the B&B and general store, cross the bridge over Laurel Hill Creek, and immediately turn right on a fisherman's trail. This trail is informal, multivalued, unmarked, and unmaintained, but it goes all the way to the base of the dam. (Most fishermen's trails only go as far as the first place the fish bite.) Along the way you will see spruces and white pines in an evergreen plantation, large white oaks, ironwoods, beeches, serviceberries, red oaks, rhododendrons, azaleas, and perhaps even a fisherman. When you reach the dam, cut left along the base, and make your way behind the beach to the concession stand. Turn left, and you are soon back in the beach parking area where you left your car.

A longer hike in Roaring Run Natural Area on the other side of Laurel Hill is described in Hike 13.

10

Whitetail Trail

Distance: 12.8 km (7.9 miles)

Time: 4½ hours

Rise: 195 meters (640 feet)

Highlight: Views

Maps: USGS 7½' Brownfield

During the early '80s the Allegheny Group of the Sierra Club blazed the Whitetail Trail as part of the Allegheny Trail. The Allegheny Trail was designed to connect the Appalachian Trail in central Virginia with the Bruce Trail in Ontario. The Whitetail Trail follows Chestnut Ridge from Quebec Run Wild Area to Lick Hollow Picnic Area on US 40, the National Pike. The portion north of Skyline Drive (Seaton Road) is entirely on public lands, consisting of State Game Land No. 138 and Forbes State Forest. This is a car shuttle hike, and hiking boots are strongly recommended.

From the west the car shuttle is easy. On US 40 east of Uniontown, leave one car at the gate on the access road to Lick Hollow Picnic Area. Do not block the gate. Even in season the gate is not opened before 11 AM. Out of season it's never opened.

If you are westbound on US 40 (four lanes at this point) *do not* attempt to turn left to the picnic area, but continue west to Hopwood. Exit there and return on US 40 east.

Next, drive east on US 40 to the top of Chestnut Ridge (1.8 miles), and then turn right on Skyline Drive, called Seaton Road on maps. (There's a large sign for Laurel Caverns.) Drive south for 3.8 miles, and park in a game commission parking lot on the right.

Pick up the blue-blazed trail at the far corner of the lot, and follow it into the woods. Some of the blue blazes are plastic rectangles nailed to trees, while others are painted on trees. You will need to follow both on this trail. At 0.6 km (0.4 mile) jog right on a jeep road,

and then continue on the trail. Next, bear left on a recent logging road at 1.1 km (0.7 mile) and follow it for 0.3 km (0.2 mile) before bearing right on the trail.

Continue on a succession of jeep roads, and cross a pipeline at 1.8 km (1.1 miles). At 2.8 km (1.7 miles) turn left on an eroded old road and descend gently, crossing the white-blazed boundary of Forbes State Forest.

Turn right in a sag at 3.1 km (1.9 miles) and descend steeply to an old logging road. Turn right again along the white-blazed forest boundary. Then turn right on a very rough and rocky trail at 3.6 km (2.2 miles), crossing several old log skids. There's no trace of sidehill construction here.

At 3.8 km (2.4 miles) bear right on an old road that proceeds east up the valley at Redstone Creek. Cross Redstone Creek as best you can at 4.6 km (2.9 miles) and follow the blazes carefully to 4.9 km (3.0 miles). Here you turn sharply right, and climb

steeply on an old grade. Pass a campsite at the top of this pitch and continue on a beautiful old road that climbs gently to the crest of this spur.

Turn left on Pine Knob Road, a dirt township road, at 6.0 km (3.7 miles). This road is not gated to traffic, as you can see from the abundant litter. Blazes are few and far between along the road, but continue north to 7.9 km (4.9 miles), where you turn right on trail at a signed junction. If you miss this turn, you'll soon reach Pine Knob Trail and a side road to the knob.

You'll come to a signed junction with Pine Knob Trail. If the day is fair, turn left at this junction, and follow this blue-blazed trail across Pine Knob Road and up to the knob. Vehicles have abused this bit of trail, producing the erosion you see. From Pine Knob you can look out over Uniontown and north along Chestnut Ridge. Curiously, there don't appear to be any pines on Pine Knob.

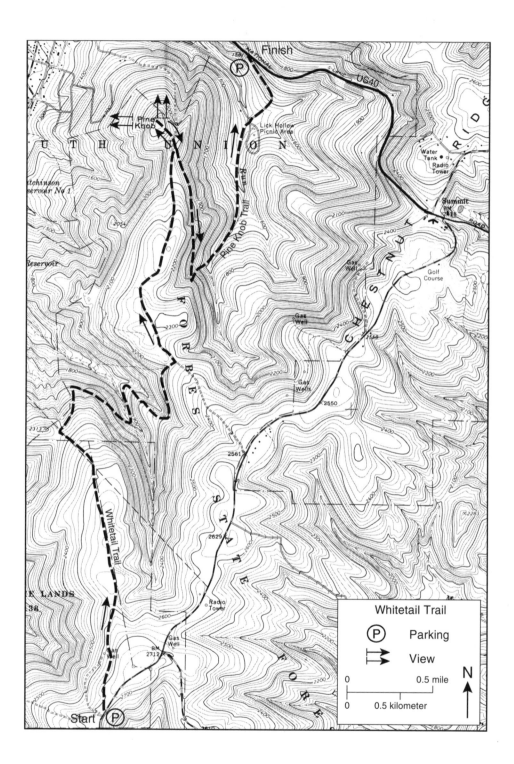

Finish

US40

RIDG

Water
Tank
Radio
Tower

Summit
BM
2418

RG40

Pine
Knob

UTH
NNION

Lick Hollow
Picnic Area

Pine Knob Trail

tchinson
servoir No 1

FORBES

Gas
Well

Golf
Course

Reservoir

Gas
Well

STATE

Gas
Wells

CHESTNUT

2550

2561

Whitetail Trail

2629

Radio
Tower

Gas
Well

FORE

E LANDS
38

Gas
Well

BM
2712

Whitetail Trail		
Ⓟ	Parking	
→	View	

0   0.5 mile

0   0.5 kilometer

N

Start Ⓟ

The abundant trash shows how popular this area is. In places the ground cover consists entirely of greenbrier.

Return the way you came, and continue down the trail to Lick Hollow on some beautiful sidehill trail. (Hardly anyone has made sidehill like this since the CCC marched off to World War II.) Watch carefully for trailing arbutus.

Switchback left at 8.9 km (5.5 miles) at the edge of a stream, and continue down over very rocky trail to 10.1 km (6.3 miles), where you bear left on an old road. Reach the parking lot near the picnic area office at 10.6 km (6.6 miles). To reach US 40 turn right, and follow the unblazed road over Lick Run and uphill to the gate on US 40.

Other hiking opportunities can be found at Quebec Run Wild Area to the south and Ohiopyle State Park to the north on PA 381.

11

Blue Hole Creek

Distance: 12.9 km (8.0 miles)

Time: 4¾ hours

Rise: 280 meters (920 feet)

Highlight: Mountain streams

Maps: USGS 7½' Seven Springs, Kingwood

This circuit hike along Blue Hole Creek is in an isolated section of Forbes State Forest on Laurel Hill, south of Seven Springs Ski Area and Resort. At one time, Blue Hole Road followed the creek all the way to Glade Road, but streams and roads have an uneasy alliance. The valley provides an easy grade for the road, though the stream may switch course in time of flood and wash out the road. This happened too many times on Blue Hole Road, and the upper portion was abandoned and blocked off to traffic. The Blue Hole itself is a deep pool in the creek, just below a rapids where Garys Run enters.

This hike is best done at the drier times of the year. The map shows the trail staying on the west side of Blue Hole Creek. Don't believe it. There are many crossings. Wear your hiking boots. And nearby Seven Springs Resort leaks mountain bikes at every crack. Watch out for them.

Blue Hole Creek can most easily be reached from PA 653 between Normalville and New Centerville. From the east, turn north on SR 3035 just after Laurel Hill Creek, and drive 1.0 mile. Then jog right on SR 3014, and turn left on Fall Run Road just before a covered bridge. From the west, turn left on SR 3014, and proceed to Fall Run Road. Turn left again, and proceed for 1.0 mile. Then take the second right. This is Blue Hole Road. Proceed upstream, passing Blue Hole at 2.2 miles, and park at the junction with Cole Run Road at 3.3 miles.

To start the hike, climb over the berm used to block the old road at this junction. Proceed up the old road, which is also blocked with an abundance of fallen trees.

The bridge over Blue Hole Creek

At 2.9 km (1.8 miles) climb over the boulders used to block this end of the old road, bear left on Glade Road, and climb hard to 3.7 km (2.3 miles), where you turn left on Pritts Distillery Road. Continue climbing, and ignore a gated road to the left. At the top of Laurel Hill turn left at a gas well, and follow another road. Turn left on the yellow-blazed Laurel Highlands Hiking Trail (LHHT), which appears to be on private land here at 4.2 km (2.6 miles). Bikes are not permitted on the LHHT.

Soon you pass the LHHT milepost 26. Cross a white-blazed boundary into Forbes State Forest at 4.9 km (3.0 miles). Next, pass milepost 25, and descend steeply on steps to cross Blue Hole Creek on a bridge at 6.5 km (4.0 miles). Then climb to 7.0 km (4.3 miles), where you turn left on a blue-blazed side trail to the Grindle Ridge shelters. (Reservations and camping fees are required to stay at the shelters.)

Continue past the water pump and rest rooms, and follow the access road out to Pletcher Road, ignoring a logging road to the left. Just beyond the gate, turn left on a gas pipeline that parallels Pletcher Road. After a couple of hundred yards the pipeline diverges to the left. Recross Garys Run as best you can, and continue along the lower edge of a logged-over tract. Then continue through uncut woods, reaching a gas well at 10.7 km (6.6 miles).

The lower edge of a clear-cut can be seen to the left. At 0.5 km (0.3 mile) there are a pair of stream crossings where part of Blue Hole Creek washed out the road.

The bridge at the forks of the Blue Hole is long gone, and even the barriers are rotting away. In low water you may be able to cross below the old bridge, but in high water detour through the brush to the left, and cross the wider fork as best you can. Then turn left on the old road, and continue up the valley, crossing a side stream and Blue Hole Creek twice. Ignore an old road coming in from the left at 2.0 km (1.2 miles). Cross Blue Hole Creek again, and ignore a road on the right, which is the old route of Glade Road.

From here on, Blue Hole Creek has taken over the road, and you are forced to swing back and forth across it. However, it is much reduced in size.

Turn left and follow the access road, which descends into the valley of Blue Hole Creek and passes through a clearing that affords views across the valley. The access road switchbacks to the right at 11.8 km (7.3 miles) and passes a sawmill site. Note the large pile of rejected slabs. Then pass a gate, bear left, and return to your car.

Other nearby hikes are at Mountain Streams (Hike 12) and Roaring Run Natural Area (Hike 13).

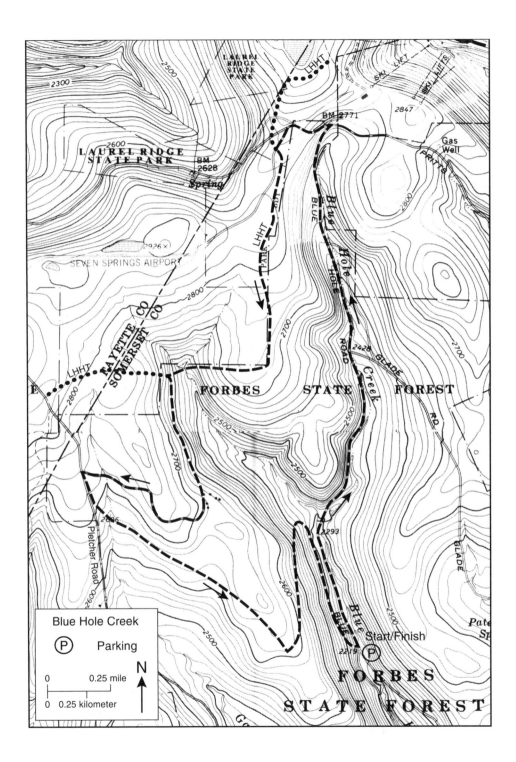

2300

2500

LAUREL
RIDGE
STATE
PARK

LHHT

SKI LIFTS

SKI LIFTS

2847

BM 2771

Gas
Well

2600

LAUREL RIDGE
STATE PARK

BM
2628

Spring

LHHT

LHHT

Blue Hole

2800

BLUE

2926 ×

SEVEN SPRINGS AIRPORT

2800

2700

2428

ROAD

GLADE

2700

Creek

LHHT

FAYETTE CO

SOMERSET CO

2800

FORBES   STATE   FOREST

2500

RD.

o

2500

2700

2500

Pletcher Road

2600

2886

2293

GLADE

2500

2600

Blue

2500

Pate
Sp

2500

Blue

Start/Finish

Blue Hole Creek

Ⓟ   Parking

0   0.25 mile

N

0   0.25 kilometer

2219

Ⓟ

FORBES

STATE   FOREST

Go

12

Mountain Streams Trail

Distance: 13.0 km (8.0 miles)

Time: 4½ hours

Rise: 345 meters (1,130 feet)

Highlight: Mountain streams

Maps: USGS 7½' Seven Springs, Bakersville

Between the Pennsylvania Turnpike and PA 31 lies another part of Forbes State Forest that used to be part of the Western Pennsylvania Conservancy's Mountain Streams Tract, like Roaring Run. This is the valley of Little Run and the surrounding ridges. It is a delight to return to a hike after many years and find that it's in better shape than before. This is the case with Mountain Streams. Roads have been improved and signed, at least parts of the trail are marked, and there are even some trail signs. Repeated stream crossings and wet spots call for hiking boots on this hike, and it should be made only at fairly low water.

To reach the trailhead, turn north on the Tunnel Road from PA 31. The junction is on the east slope of Laurel Hill, just 0.3 mile west of Hidden Valley Ski Area and directly across from an active stone quarry. Drive north on the Tunnel Road, crossing the Laurel Highlands Hiking Trail, for 1.5 miles to a junction with Sky View Road. (Since the sign board wouldn't stretch, the sign calls it Sky Road.) Park along the side of the road in the next 0.4 mile, passing a springhouse on the left. Tunnel Road has been improved and carries a lot of traffic, so make sure your car is well off the road but doesn't block any gates. (The tunnel referred to is probably the old Pennsylvania Turnpike tunnel under Laurel Mountain.)

To start the hike, continue along Tunnel Road to a trail on the left opposite a gated road that is the second crossing of the North Woods ski trail. Turn left, dodge around the vehicle gate, and in a few steps turn right on Mountain Streams Trail. This trail is blazed

Boulders block the jeep road

with red markers nailed to trees. Proceed through a small meadow, and continue along an old jeep road. Soon you cross a pair of natural gas pipelines. Along this section the trail markers were removed, even the nails, but the nail holes are still there. Actually the jeep road is well defined and makes only gradual turns, so it's easy to follow even without the markers.

At 1.7 km (1.1 miles) the trail passes through an old meadow that now is filled with goldenrod and hawthorn. This old road doesn't have a sufficiently constant grade to have been a railroad. Bear left at 3.3 km (2.1 miles) where a woods road comes in from the right.

The Pennsylvania Turnpike is in the next valley to the north, and you can hear its muted roar along this part of the Mountain Streams Trail. Bear left again at 4.3 km (2.7 miles) where another woods road comes in from the right, and ignore a trail from the right at 4.6 km (2.9 miles). By now Mountain

Streams Trail is on the crest of the ridge, and individual trucks can be heard on the turnpike. The old road becomes increasingly eroded with ledges of bedrock. A rhododendron-covered ledge is to the left.

At 5.8 km (3.6 miles) you cross an old logging railroad (probably Blair Brothers Railroad), and continue downhill to turn left on another railroad grade along Indian Creek. Note the cinders in the railroad bed. At 6.3 km (3.9 miles) cross Little Run on a new footbridge. Turn left on Little Run Trail at 6.7 km (4.2 miles), just before reaching a low ridge. There are no trail signs and no markers on Little Run Trail, but it's an old woods road in good condition and easy to follow. Pass a boulder bar, intended to stop ATVs, and avoid a trail to the right just 100 meters (about 300 feet) farther on. After climbing a bit, the trail turns right and runs along the side of Little Run on an old logging railroad grade. Little Run tumbles over moss-covered rocks as it flows among the

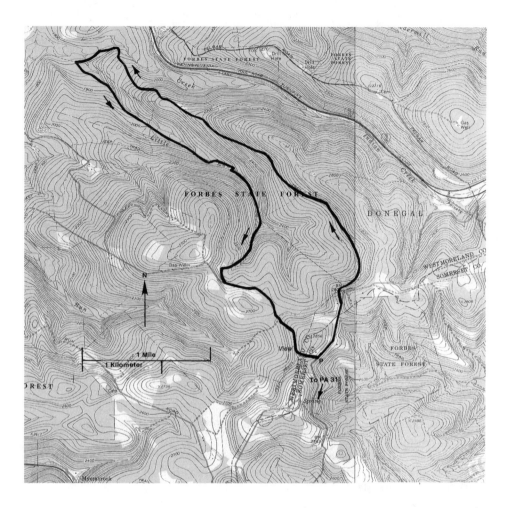

rhododendrons. Even after months of drought it still has a good flow since it drains a wooded watershed.

At 7.7 km (4.8 miles) there are a pair of crossings of Little Run. Look for ruins of the old railroad bridge at the first crossing. At 8.1 km (5.0 miles) avoid a trail to the right. Next, cross a side stream and then Little Run two more times. At 8.6 km (5.3 miles) pass a trail to the left, and then keep right to avoid crossing Little Run. There is little temptation to follow any of these side trails; they may have been formed by ATV drivers showing what steep slopes they could ride

without actually killing themselves. Next, ignore a trail to the right, and cross Little Run at 8.9 km (5.5 miles). Then ignore two more trails to the right and one to the left, and cross Little Run again.

At 9.3 km (5.8 miles) leave the old railroad grade, and turn right into an abandoned gas well clearing. Continue across the goldenrod-covered clearing and follow the access road and pipeline up the valley. The old railroad grade can still be seen along Little Run to the left.

At 10.1 km (6.3 miles) cross Little Run again and in another 100 meters (about

300 feet) turn right on a gas line road. Cross Little Run for the last time on a culvert, pass a steel pipe gate, now disabled, and then bear right on another gas line road. This road climbs out of Little Run Valley by way of a hollow to the south. Partway up, keep left where the road splits. Near the top the road bears left in an old clearing that has been invaded by hawthorns and crab apples. After passing a boulder barrier and the ruins of a gate, turn left on little-used Sky View Road at 11.3 km (7.0 miles).

At 12.2 km (7.6 miles) pass a gated road right into a large clear-cut, followed by a stiff climb to the top of Laurel Ridge, where the road turns right along the top of the clear-cut. Turn left at 12.7 km (7.9 miles) to avoid a private road ahead, cross a pipeline, and follow the road back to Tunnel Road just over the summit. Turn left along Tunnel Road to reach your car.

Additional hiking opportunities can be found at Roaring Run south of PA 31 (Hike 13), Laurel Hill State Park (Hike 9), and the Kincora Trail at Kooser State Park, just down the hill on PA 31.

13

Roaring Run Natural Area

Distance: 13.2 km (8.2 miles)

Time: 5 Hours

Rise: 375 meters (1,230 feet)

Highlights: Mountain stream; spring wildflowers

Map: USGS 7½' Seven Springs; State Forest Natural Area map

At 1,450 hectares (3,582 acres) Roaring Run is the largest state forest natural area in western Pennsylvania. It is part of the mountain streams tract that was purchased by the Western Pennsylvania Conservancy on the western slopes of Laurel Ridge and transferred to Forbes State Forest in 1975. Before the conservancy acquired the tract, a good deal of logging had been carried out. It will take a century for the second- and third-growth hardwood forest to mature, but hikers of the late 21st century have a real treat in store.

The trailhead can be reached entirely on paved roads. Owing to frequent crossings of Roaring Run, this hike should be attempted only during low water, and hiking boots and long pants to protect your legs from catbriers and other briers are a must. The best time to visit Roaring Run for spring wildflowers is the last two weeks in April.

To reach the trailhead from PA 31, turn south on PA 381 and PA 711 at Jones Mills. After 1.2 miles turn left on County Line Road (SR 1058) at the gas station in Champion. Then go 1.9 miles to a small parking area on the left side of the road.

To start your hike, walk around the boulder, and head up the old woods road. Much of this hike is on similar old roads. The natural area is closed to motor vehicles, and the trail is marked with red blazes.

At 0.5 km (0.3 mile) you continue ahead where the South Loop Trail comes in from the right. Farther on, the old road crosses a culvert over a small stream. Catbriers flourish in the undergrowth along this section. They can make off-trail hiking very painful but are a

favorite food of deer. Where the trail cuts across a steep slope, note the boulders that have slid down the mountain.

At 1.5 km (0.9 mile) you pass an intersection with the Painter Rock Trail, and then cross Roaring Run. (This is the first of 28 stream crossings, and if this one does not appear feasible, you had best retreat and just hike up and back on the South Loop Trail.) Turn right, and continue up Roaring Run.

After the second stream crossing, look for rhododendrons growing along the run. They should bloom in early July. The straightness of the trail along Roaring Run shows it was a logging railroad. Near 2.3 km (1.4 miles) look for a basswood tree growing along the run. Basswood can be recognized by its nearly circular or heart-shaped leaves and its seeds, which are borne in a cluster attached to a narrow leaflike blade or sail. Although basswood is classed as a hardwood, its wood is actually soft and suitable for carving. Iroquois Indians

carved masks from a living tree; when the outside of each mask was finished, it was split off to hollow out the back. Using live wood increased the medicine or spiritual power of the mask.

A small meadow is reached at 2.8 km (1.7 miles) and next you cross two small streams from the south. After this, the crossings of Roaring Run become more frequent. At about 4 km (2.5 miles) the trail really starts to climb, and the stream is much reduced in size. There is a double crossing at 4.8 km (3.0 miles). These two crossings are some of the very few on this hike that could be avoided without excessive bushwhacking. The next eight crossings come in quick order as the valley is constricted by steep banks.

At 5.4 km (3.3 miles) multiple blazes announce the junction with the Painter Rock Trail. There's also a campsite near the stream. (If you miss the Painter Rock Trail, you will next meet the even more obscure junction with the South Loop and then reach a parking

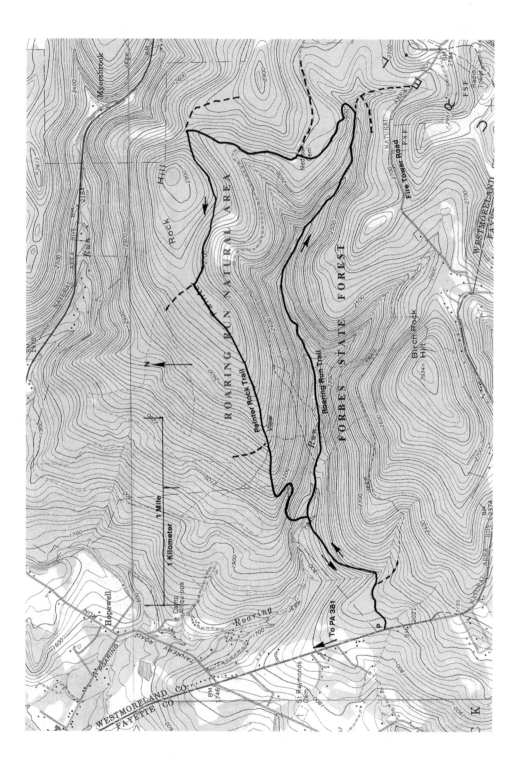

lot on the Fire Tower Road.) Turn left on the Painter Rock Trail, which is also red-blazed, and cross Roaring Run once again. Next, turn sharp left, and climb the stream bank on a rough footway. At the top of the hill the footway improves, and soon you pick up an old woods road that leads to a clearing.

Just beyond the clearing a cross-country ski trail comes in from the right on a jeep road. The Painter Rock Trail continues ahead on this jeep road. At 6.6 km (4.1 miles) there is a marker to the right of the trail for D. A. Sheets, C. K. Baker, and Catherine Saylor, who were killed on January 19, 1896 in a sleigh accident on their way home from church.

At 7.1 km (4.4 miles) keep right on the Painter Rock and McKenna Trails. Continue to the top of the ridge and a junction where the McKenna Trail turns right. Turn left here on the Painter Rock Trail, and follow the red blazes around the high point of Painter Rock Hill on an old woods road.

At 8.5 km (5.3 miles) bear right, and follow blue blazes uphill. The red-blazed cross-country ski trail turns sharp left downhill on an old woods road. Continue uphill to a junction with the North Loop Trail (also blue-blazed) at 8.8 km (5.5 miles).

Turn left at this unsigned junction, and continue on the Painter Rock Trail along an old woods road. At 9.5 km (5.9 miles) bear left on a less-well-defined woods road. Then turn left again onto rocky trail at 9.7 km (6.0 miles). Next you pass a small cliff to the left as catbrier begins to encroach on the trail. At 10.5 km (6.5 miles) you reach a view over Roaring Run from the brink of a cliff. This is where your long pants earn their keep.

Before you reach another junction with the North Loop at 10.8 km (6.7 miles) the catbrier has generally receded from the trail. Continue downhill along the edge of Painter Rock Hill, and then follow the trail down a series of rough switchbacks to a last crossing of Roaring Run at 11.6 km (7.2 miles). A few meters beyond the run, turn right on the Roaring Run Trail, and retrace your steps for 1.5 km (0.9 mile) to your car.

Other hiking opportunities in the Roaring Run Natural Area are the South Loop, which forms a circuit across the slopes of Birch Rock Hill, and the McKenna Trail, which leads out to Fire Tower Road near PA 31. Your hike could be greatly extended by using the North Loop Trail. Also the Laurel Highlands Hiking Trail crosses the southeastern corner of the natural area.

14

Bear Run Nature Reserve

Distance: 14.3 km (8.8 miles)

Time: 5¼ hours

Rise: 355 meters (1,160 feet)

Highlights: Wildflowers; mountain streams; views

Maps: USGS 7½' Mill Run; Bear Run Trail map (frequently available at trailhead and from Western Pennsylvania Conservancy)

Normally, the Western Pennsylvania Conservancy transfers acquired lands to public ownership. There is one area, however, that the conservancy chose to keep—the Bear Run Nature Reserve. The conservancy has expanded the original tract surrounding Fallingwater, the famous house designed by Frank Lloyd Wright, to 1400 hectares (3,460 acres). The reserve stretches from the banks of the Youghiogheny far up the western flank of Laurel Hill and encompasses most of the watersheds of both Laurel Run and Bear Run itself. Almost 32 kilometers (20 miles) of trails lace the reserve, which is open to nonmembers for both day hiking and overnight camping. Users of the backpack campsites should register at the parking lot. Reservations are required for the lone group campsite (10 or more campers).

This hike takes you on a grand tour of the trails at Bear Run, through dense woods, pine plantations, and rhododendron thickets, across fields, and along mountain streams to a view of rafts and kayaks knocking the rocks out of the lower Yough. The many rocks and wet areas call for hiking boots. There are several ways this hike can be shortened.

Bear Run Nature Reserve is on PA 381 about 4 miles north of Ohiopyle and 3.5 miles south of Mill Run. Drive in at the sign, and park in the large lot behind the nature center. The hike begins at the far end of the parking lot.

Head into the pine plantation on the Wagon Trail. Almost immediately the Pine Trail takes off to the left, and very shortly

junction of the Laurel Run and Tulip Tree Trails.) At 1.0 km (0.6 mile) the Hemlock Trail goes off to the right. Other trees found along this section are red oak, tulip, black gum, chestnut oak, cucumber, black birch, red maple, and the much smaller striped maple. At 1.7 km (1.1 miles) bear left where the Hemlock Trail comes back in from the right, and left again at 1.9 km (1.2 miles) where the old road goes straight ahead.

Teaberry Trail comes in from the left at 2.0 km (1.2 miles). Along this section you can see sassafras and beech trees as well as mountain laurel. Backpack campsite 2 is found at 3.4 km (2.1 miles). At 3.8 km (2.4 miles) you reach a junction with the Rhododendron, Bear Run, and Tulip Tree Trails. Continue straight ahead on the Tulip Tree Trail, which is also blazed with yellow spots. In late May, look for the pink lady's-slipper. At 4.1 km (2.6 miles) watch the blazes as the Tulip Tree Trail makes an obscure jog to the left near some large rocks. For the most part, the Tulip Tree Trail is fairly faint and requires careful attention, particularly at junctions with other old woods roads.

Soon the trail begins descending, and at 5.6 km (3.5 miles) you reach the junction with the Snowbunny Trail. This is your last chance to return to the parking lot without going around the large inholding of private land or walking back on the highway. Continue ahead on the white-blazed Laurel Run Trail, and another 0.4 km (0.2 mile) brings you to a crossing of Laurel Run itself, which you follow along until you reach the edge of a field. Turn left and pick up a trail that takes you down to PA 381 at 7.0 km (4.3 miles). Follow blazes carefully, or you could wind up on an old road overgrown with briers.

Cross the highway and continue downhill. Soon you turn left, cross Laurel Run, pass through a rhododendron tunnel, and

the Arbutus Trail diverges to the right. In theory the Wagon Trail is blazed with orange rectangles, but the trail is wide and well used and the blazing correspondingly scarce. Next, the Poetry Trail goes off to your right. The white pine trees along the Wagon Trail give way to red pine. After the Aspen Trail, which goes left, you come to spruce.

At 0.8 km (0.5 mile) the Wagon Trail comes to an end, and you turn left on the Ridge Trail blazed with yellow spots. Rhododendron thickets and white oaks border the trail at this point. Shortly, you cross a bridge over Beaver Run, and the Arbutus Trail comes in from the right. Listen for the song of the wood thrush. Next, the white-blazed Rhododendron Trail goes off to the left. (One way to shorten this hike and avoid over 90 meters (almost 300 feet) of climbing would be to take the Rhododendron and Snowbunny Trails to the

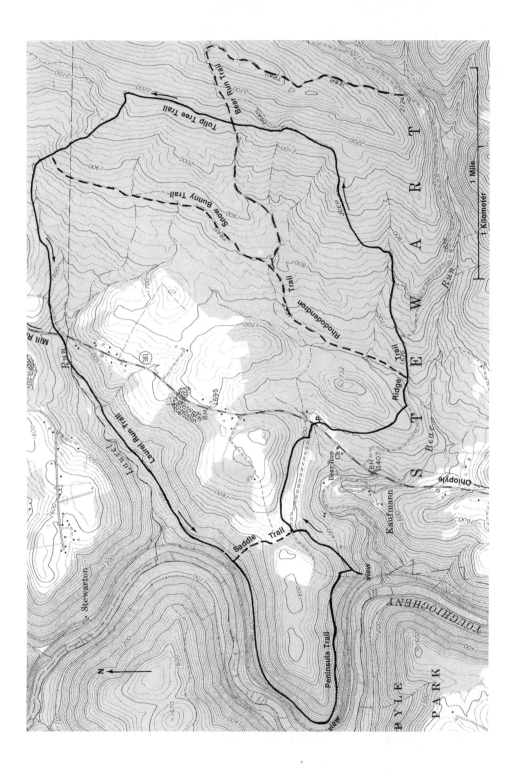

climb into more open woods above the stream. Next, the trail returns to the side of Laurel Run at the ruins of a dam. Just beyond, a spur trail leads right to a view of lower Laurel Glen before returning to the main trail. Then the trail climbs away from Laurel Run, picks up an old road grade, emerges into the lower Yough gorge, and swings upstream, following the old road far above the river. At 9.5 km (5.9 miles) you reach a junction with the orange-blazed Saddle Trail, which if you took it would shorten your hike but would also bypass the overlook on the Yough at the west end of the peninsula.

Just beyond this junction you pass campsite 4 to the right of the trail. At 10.6 km (6.6 miles) the trail picks up a pole line. At times the trail follows an old quarry above the pole line. At 11.6 km (7.3 miles), however, you emerge at an overlook that makes it all worthwhile. You're about 20 meters (about 65 feet) directly above the main line of the Baltimore & Ohio Railroad. You get a good view of the river at Dimple Rapids and can watch the kayaks and rafts dodging the many rocks. You probably heard the screams and shouts from below as you hiked the Peninsula Trail, but now you can actually see what is going on.

Back on the Peninsula Trail you traverse the slope for the next 0.9 km (0.6 mile) on a trail cut by the Keystone Trails Association Trail Care team in 1988. At 12.4 km (7.8 miles) you reach the Daniel G. Paradise Memorial Overlook at the brink of an impressive cliff. Continuing on the Peninsula Trail, you climb to the edge of a field where you turn right, and the Saddle Trail comes in from the left. At the far edge of the field, you can vary the walk back by turning left on the yellow-blazed Kinglet Trail or continuing on the Peninsula Trail. In either case, it's about 0.8 km (0.5 mile) back to PA 381, just across from the entrance to the Bear Run parking lot.

As this hike uses less than half the trails in Bear Run Nature Reserve, there are plenty of opportunities for further hiking. As mentioned earlier, Fallingwater, the famous house designed by Frank Lloyd Wright, is near at hand, and well worth a visit (for further information call 724-329-1441). To reach Fallingwater, turn south on PA 381 for 0.5 mile, and then turn right at the sign.

15

Quebec Run Wild Area

Distance: 14.4 km (8.9 miles)

Time: 5 hours

Rise: 295 meters (960 feet)

Highlights: Wild areas; mountain streams

Maps: USGS 7½' Bruceton Mills,
Brownfield; State Forest Wild Area map

The Quebec Run Wild Area is a heavily forested section of land in Forbes State Forest on the eastern slope of Chestnut Ridge, just a tad north of the Mason-Dixon Line. Chestnut Ridge, like Laurel Ridge, is an anticline. Layers of rock have gently folded to form a great arch. It helps to have the topmost layer a hard one, resistant to erosion. The hard upper layer of Chestnut Ridge is Pottsville sandstone. This stone is of great significance in Pennsylvania because all the commercial coal seams lie above it. There are a few traces of Devonian coal below, but they are of interest primarily to geologists.

The trailhead for Quebec Run Wild Area is most easily reached from US 40 east of Uniontown. Turn south at the top of Chestnut Ridge on Skyline Drive (SR 2001, called Seaton Road on the map), just east of the Mount Summit Inn. Follow the signs for Laurel Caverns, but continue past the cavern turnoff. Bypass the road to Pondfield Fire Tower. At 6.6 miles from US 40, turn left on the Quebec Road, called Mud Pike on the map, for 2.5 miles more, passing the north parking lot to another parking lot just before Mill Run.

The hike starts off from the parking lot on the blue-blazed Mill Run Trail, which follows the run mostly at water level but climbs the bank to avoid steep spots.

Chestnut Ridge was named for the American chestnut, which sprouts abundantly along this trail. The chestnut was a versatile tree. In town its spreading branches provided shade, while in the forest it grew straight and tall for timber. Its

Looking downstream on Mill Run

beautiful wood was suitable for both rough and fine construction, and since it resisted rot, it was used for fence posts, too. When the tree was cut, the stump would resprout vigorously, and the nuts provided food for both wildlife and humans. At the turn of the century the American chestnut comprised about half of the trees in the Appalachians from Maine to Georgia. These forests were then decimated by a fungal blight (*Endothia parasitica*), which may have been introduced in a shipment of trees or logs from Europe. The fungus killed the aboveground portion of the trees, but the roots were not affected, and today, some 90 years later, they continue to send up healthy shoots. Although some of these shoots grow large enough to bear nuts, they eventually contract the blight and die.

At 1.7 km (1.1 miles) you pass a junction with the Miller Trail, and at 2.0 km (1.2 miles) reach a junction with the Ran-kin Trail on which you'll return. Continue on Mill Run Trail, crossing the Pennsylvania Conservation Corps bridge over Quebec Run.

Look for deer tracks in the mud. I found two sets, one full-sized, the other diminutive. The tracks were so fresh and sharp that I suspect the deer were moving down the trail directly ahead of me, just far enough in front to keep out of sight.

Next, you return to the edge of Mill Run. A modular truss bridge of the Drexel design has been built across Mill Run at this spot. It connects with the Grist Mill Trail on the east side of Mill Run, and you will cross it later in this hike. Pass it by for now, and continue downstream on Mill Run Trail, sometimes right along Mill Run and at others out of sight of the stream. The old railroad grade is used whenever it's on the west side, but frequently it's on the east side. You cross many side streams, some small and some

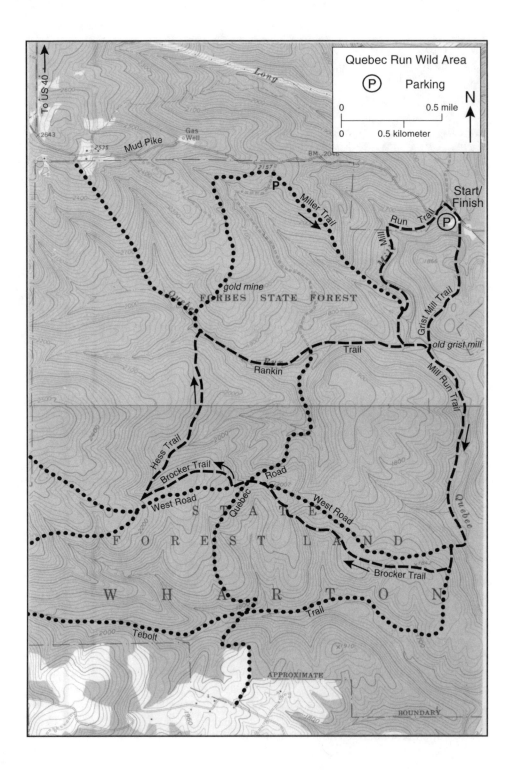

Quebec Run Wild Area

P Parking

0   0.5 mile
0   0.5 kilometer

N

To US 40

Long

Mud Pike

Gas
Well

2643

2535

2600

2700

2400

2500

BM 2046

2157

P

Miller Trail

Start/
Finish

Mill
Run Trail

P

gold mine

FORBES STATE FOREST

1866

Grist Mill Trail

old grist mill

Rankin   Trail

Mill Run Trail

Hess Trail

Brocker Trail

Road

2500

West Road

Quebec

West Road

Quebec

S T A T E

F O R E S T L A N D

Brocker Trail

W H A R T O N

1910

Tebolt   Trail

APPROXIMATE

BOUNDARY

rather large. Turn right on the West Road at 4.5 km (2.9 miles) and start the long climb up the flank of Chestnut Ridge. At 4.7 km (2.9 miles) turn left on the Tebolt Trail, and continue to climb, but more gently, as you follow it through a small meadow.

You reach the Brocker Trail at 5.0 km (3.1 miles) and turn right on it through a stand of larch, or tamarack, trees. At 5.6 km (3.5 miles) you cross the Tebolt Road. Continue ahead on the Brocker Trail, crossing a ravine and the traces of several old logging roads, to the Quebec road at 7.1 km (4.4 miles). Cross the Quebec Road and continue on the West Road. Soon, you turn right on the relocated Brocker Trail. Follow the Brocker Trail to its junction with the Hess Trail. Turn right on the Hess Trail, which takes you downhill on an old road along a stream. You cross this stream and then another. Bear left on a relocation trail cut in September 1999. Descend into a rhododendron jungle and turn right along a branch of Quebec Run. Immediately up the bank, cross Quebec Run at 10.3 km (6.4 miles) and bear right on the Rankin Trail, passing junctions with the old Hess Trail. Follow the Rankin downstream, passing cascades in the stream below and also some large rocks to the left.

Cross Quebec Road at 11.2 km (6.9 miles) and continue downstream, crossing Quebec Run twice on bridges built by the Pennsylvania Conservation Corps. At the junction with Mill Run Trail turn right, recrossing Quebec Run. This time take the bridge over Mill Run, turn right and pass between the stone ruins of the gristmill and the remains of the millrace. Note where the shaft from the waterwheel entered the building.

At 12.7 km (7.9 miles) you reach a critical junction. Turn left on the Grist Mill Trail. Note that this trail goes in both directions. Climb slowly to a height-of-land. Watch the blazes carefully for a sharp turn to the left. Avoid an unblazed trail with an obvious footway that continues ahead. The Grist Mill Trail descends along a ravine, crossing it farther along. Turn left on Quebec Road, and cross the bridge over Mill Run to your car.

Backpacking is permitted in the Quebec Run Wild Area, but you should obtain a camping permit from the forest head-quarters back at Pondfield Tower on Skyline Drive.

The Rankin Trail, Tebolt Trail, and Quebec Road provide alternatives that could be used to either lengthen or shorten this hike. For a cool hike underground, you could visit Laurel Caverns.

16

New Florence Game Lands

Distance: 16.9 km (10.5 miles)

Time: 5¼ hours

Rise: 510 meters (1,680 feet)

Highlights: Laurel Highlands Trail; iron furnace

Maps: USGS 7½' Rachel Wood; Hiker's Guide to the Laurel Highlands Trail, *map 11*

In the western part of the state there are over 100,000 hectares (almost 250,00 acres) of state game lands. Next to the lands of the Allegheny National Forest they are the most abundant type of public lands. Yet these lands have few marked trails. The Laurel Highlands Trail traverses State Game Lands Nos. 111 and 42, while the Baker Trail passes through State Game Lands Nos. 24, 283, and 74. Since the Pennsylvania Game Commission is supported primarily by hunting license fees, you can understand why it tries to serve hunters rather than hikers.

This hike is located in the largest of four tracts comprising State Game Land No. 42, on the west flank of Laurel Hill, above the small town of New Florence (named after Firenze in Italy). You will see evidence of past industrial activity on Laurel Hill. It hasn't always been as wild as it is today.

The trailhead is the Pennsylvania Game Commission parking lot at the end of the road from New Florence. New Florence is 7.7 miles south of US 22 via PA 56 and PA 711. At the south edge of town, turn east on Furnace Lane. Continue straight ahead at a stop sign 0.8 mile from PA 711. Turn right at 1.0 mile, and pass a large charcoal iron furnace. The parking lot and end of the road are at 1.7 miles. Due to the length of this hike, hiking boots are the choice.

To start the hike, squeeze around the gate, and proceed to a cluster of storage buildings. Just beyond the large garage turn left, cross a bridge over Baldwin Creek, and start up the gravel management road called

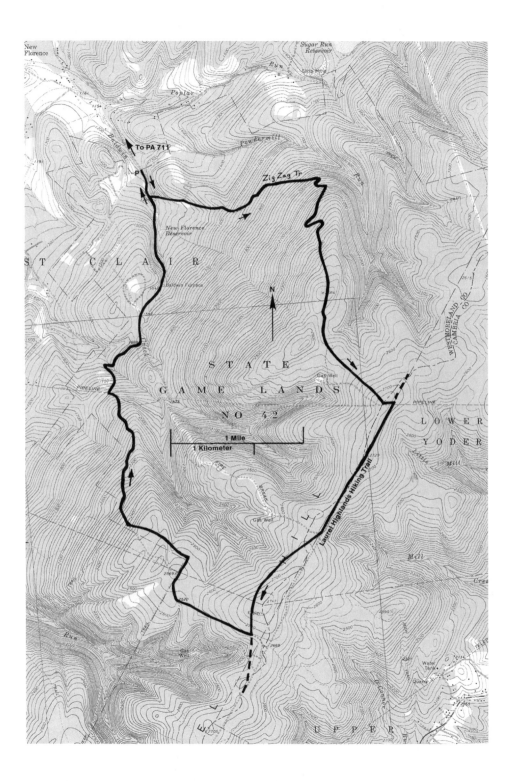

Zig Zag. The road is marked with occasional orange diamonds showing this road is a snowmobile trail in season (January 15 to April 15). Soon you reach a small meadow on your right, but avoid a road to your left that dead ends at some game food plots. At 0.8 km (0.5 mile) you reach the corner of a clear-cut made in 1978. This clear-cut has greened up and is returning to forest.

At 1.6 km (1.0 mile) avoid a road to the right that leads uphill to some more recent clear-cuts. You reach the first of a series of switchbacks at 2.4 km (1.5 miles). There are five switchbacks in all as you continue to make your way up the flank of Laurel Hill. The last two switchbacks are in a gypsy moth salvage cut.

At 3.8 km (2.4 miles) the climbing eases off, but the region of damage from the gypsy moth infestation in the mid-'80s continues. This is a selective timber cut. Healthy trees were left to seed in a new generation of forest, but it isn't revegetating very well. There weren't many trees that the gypsy moths didn't like. Trees on a ridgetop are stressed because there may not be a water table, which is why gypsy moth damage was so bad on ridgetops. Today a virus and a fungus seem to keep these moths in check, and seedlings have been planted in plastic tubes to protect them from the deer. The tubes also conserve moisture, and the seedlings may grow twice as fast as they would in the open.

At 5.7 km (3.6 miles) pass a gate and continue. Turn left at 6.2 km (3.8 miles) on the swath of a major pipeline. After just 100 meters (300 feet), turn right on the yellow-blazed Laurel Highlands Trail, which follows another major pipeline at this point.

Through this section, the Laurel Highlands Trail is out in the open on the service road along the pipeline. The adjacent portion of the game lands is a wildlife refuge. Not only is hunting prohibited within the refuge, but the hiking trail has also been excluded. The yellow blazes are on wooden posts along the border of the pipeline swath. An old clear-cut is to the left on private land that seems to be coming back to witch hazel. It permits views over the eastern flank of Laurel Ridge.

At 8.1 km (5.0 miles) another management road comes in from the right, and the Laurel Highlands Trail bears right into the woods. A lot of mountain laurel grows along this section. It even approaches central Pennsylvania densities. There is also a stand of black gum trees that turn the woods crimson in early fall. At 9.4 km (5.8 miles) you pass milepost 60.

At 9.8 km (6.1 miles) turn right on another management road known as the Adams Trail, but don't look for any signs. This road has been graveled all the way to a new gas well. Follow the road to the corner of Rachel Wood Game Preserve at 11.2 km (6.9 miles), a private game preserve. From this point you can see what foresters call "site conversion" in progress. Not only have large areas been clear-cut, but the slash has been burned. Conversion of the woods to meadows should increase the carrying capacity for the game animals, some of them exotic, stocked at Rachel Wood.

Turn left along the fence, and follow the management road, which soon passes the gas well. Keep left, and the Adams Trail finally reverts to its old grassy self. After crossing a low ridge, your way continues mostly down, steeply in some places but also leveling off from time to time.

You pass an old selective cut, and at one point the bedrock itself outcrops in the road. At 13.8 km (8.6 miles) bear left and cross a natural gas pipeline. Then continue down, passing game food plots. Switchback sharply to the right, and then cross a bridge over Shannon Run. The stream is bordered with hemlocks and rhododendrons.

At 14.8 km (9.2 miles) turn left on another management road. Rhododendrons grow along this road as you approach Baldwin Creek, making this section particularly attractive. Ignore a road to the left, and pass Baldwin Iron Furnace to the right, evidence of past industrial activity. A small pond—New Florence Reservoir—can be seen to the right at 16.4 km (10.2 miles) and soon you go by an old mine or quarry on the left.

Pass a road from the right, and reach the game commission storage buildings at 16.7 km (10.4 miles). Continue ahead, and you are soon back at your car.

Other nearby hiking opportunities are Conemaugh Gorge and Charles F. Lewis Natural Area (Hike 6).

17

Maple Summit to Ohiopyle

Distance: 18.0 km (11.3 miles)

Time: 6¼ Hours

Rise: 520 meters (1,700 feet)

Highlight: Views

Maps: USGS 7½' Mill Run, Ohiopyle; Hiker's Guide to the Laurel Highlands Trail, maps 1 and 2; Laurel Ridge State Park map

Laurel Ridge is a giant arch of gently folded rock—an anticline. Like Chestnut Ridge, its cap is composed of a layer of Pottsville sandstone, which resists erosion.This sandstone lies under the Ohiopyle waterfall, then rises gently upward—about 500 meters (or 1,650 feet)—to form Laurel Ridge. This is a modest anticline compared to some in the ridge-and-valley region to the east, which appear to have exceeded 9,000 meters (29,500 feet). But Laurel Ridge has survived more or less intact, whereas the ridge-and-valley anticlines have been leveled by erosion.

The Youghiogheny River has cut a water gap through Laurel Ridge, making this southernmost section of the Laurel Highlands Trail one of the most scenic. For much of its length the top of Laurel Ridge is broad and relatively flat, so views and overlooks are rare. The section between Ohiopyle and Maple Summit also contains one of the longest climbs on the Laurel Highlands Trail. While this hike is arranged so that you go down this hill, the north flank of Youghiogheny Gorge still requires several steep climbs.

To do this hike you need a car shuttle, or preferably a drop-off service. At the time of this writing, however, none of the outfitters at Ohiopyle provide this service for hikers. If that is still the case, you must either make your own drop-off arrangements or use a car shuttle. Leave one car in a lot in Ohiopyle, and drive north on PA 381 in the other car. At 1.9 miles north of the bridge, turn right on SR 2017 and drive up the flank

View across the valley of the Ohiopyle

of Laurel Ridge. After 4.0 miles more, turn right again at a sign for Confluence. It's another 1.8 miles to the obscure trail crossing. There is no parking at the crossing, but a game commission parking lot is on the left just 0.1 mile farther, and a short blue-blazed side trail to the Laurel Highlands Trail leaves from the lot. Overnight parking is not permitted at the game commission lot. However, there are shelters on this section of the trail, so this hike could be turned into a two-day backpack if you can make drop-off arrangements. Reservations are required for use of the shelters. Call 724-455-3744.

Whether you do this as a day hike or as a backpack, hiking boots are strongly recommended. As yet there are no user fees for day hikers on the Laurel Highlands Trail, but day hikers are required to register at the trailhead.

Head south along the yellow-blazed Laurel Highlands Trail. Despite the substantial split-log bridges at the many wet spots, there is still a good deal of water on this section of trail. At 1.5 km (0.9 mile) you cross Little Glade Run and begin a gentle climb toward the western edge of Laurel Hill. After passing some big rocks, you reach milepost 10. (At one time there was a complete set of these mileposts, but vandals have destroyed the ones near road crossings.) Next you pass along the base of a small cliff on your right, and at 2.8 km (1.7 miles) you cross a jeep road in a cleared swath. This road appears to service several natural gas wells. Anticlines like Laurel Ridge are textbook traps for oil and gas. Alex Run is crossed at 3.7 km (2.3 miles), and shortly you reach milepost 9. Next you approach the edge of Laurel Ridge.

The trail continues close to the western edge, past milepost 8. At 6.2 km (3.8 miles) there are several obvious side trails out to views. You can see Laurel Hill dropping away into the Youghiogheny Gorge.

Soon you start down the great descent into the Youghiogheny Gorge. Twice you cross another jeep road that leads to some natural gas wells. At 7.0 km (4.4 miles) you bear right on an old road, and pass milepost 7. There is a view over Camp Run Ravine as you continue to descend. Shortly you pass a white-blazed boundary between State Game Land No. 111 and Ohiopyle State Park.

A side trail goes left to the Camp Run shelters at 8.1 km (5.0 miles). If you've never seen a Laurel Highlands Trail shelter, take the time to inspect one. The built-in fireplace gives lots of heat. There is a well here for drinking water and also pit toilets, including one for the handicapped.

Back on the Laurel Highlands Trail, at the bottom of the great descent there is a meadow. At 8.5 km (5.3 miles) you cross a jeep road and Lick Run. The trail continues in and out of meadows to 9.5 km (5.9 miles),

where you cross a nameless stream. This is followed by a good stiff climb that continues past milepost 5. You follow along the hillside high above the Yough with occasional views of the other side of the gorge. At 11.8 km (7.4 miles) you come to milepost 4, above the large bend in the Yough that encloses the Flats. There is a fair amount of open meadow along this section. At 12.5 km (7.8 miles) you cross Rock Spring Run and begin another climb that continues almost to milepost 3.

The Laurel Highlands Trail has saved the best for the last. At 14.5 km (9.1 miles) you come to the edge of cliffs with spectacular views of the Yough and equally spectacular drops to the rocks below. Be careful. There are no guardrails.

From here the trail leads downward until it is just above the Baltimore & Ohio tracks. A giant boulder is passed at 16.5 km (10.3 miles), then milepost 1. There are clear signs of a forest fire along this section. Next you cross Sheepskin Run and then

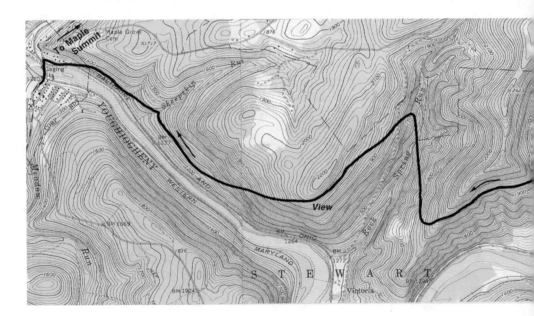

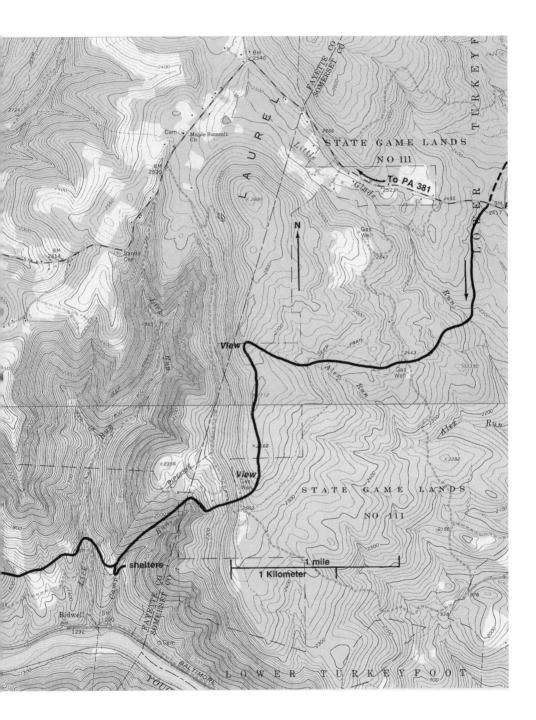

another run. A trail at 17.2 km (10.8 miles) leads right to the hiker parking lot.

The Laurel Highlands Trail shortly bears left off an old road, descends, and turns right onto a jeep road along the Baltimore & Ohio tracks. Continue into the outskirts of Ohiopyle, and 18.0 km (11.3 miles) brings you to PA 381. Turn left, cross the bridge, and reach downtown Ohiopyle.

There are other hikes at Ohiopyle State Park and nearby Bear Run Nature Preserve. See Hikes 2 (Ferncliff Natural Area), 3 (Meadow Run), 8 (Cucumber Falls), and 14 (Bear Run Nature Preserve).

II

Allegheny National Forest

18

Hearts Content Scenic Area

Distance: 1.8 km (1.1 miles)

Time: ¾ hour

Rise: 35 meters (110 feet)

Highlights: Virgin timber; log display; wheelchair accessible in part

Maps: USGS 7½' Cherry Grove, Cobham

White pine was the most valuable tree growing in Penn's Woods during the 19th-century logging era. But white pine doesn't belong to the region's climax vegetation. It is, instead, an opportunistic tree that grows in large stands following some disaster to the mature forest, such as a windstorm or fire. The great stands of white pine that the 19th-century loggers exploited in Pennsylvania are attributed to the fires of 1644. By then colonists were settled along the Atlantic Coast, and they wrote home all summer about the poor air quality as the smoke from many forest fires rolled out of the interior.

This white pine made Pennsylvania first in timber production after the Civil War. Production continued to rise until late in the 19th century. But by then several midwestern states had passed Pensylvania in timber output.

At Hearts Content a small tract of white pine has been preserved much as the loggers found it. Unlike many other small tracts of virgin lumber in Pennsylvania the circumstances are well known. In 1922 the firm of Wheeler and Dusenbury donated 8 hectares (about 20 acres) to the government. In 1931 another 40 hectares (100 acres) were purchased by the federal government, bringing the Hearts Content Scenic Area to its present size.

An interpretive audio tape for Hearts Content can be checked out at the Bradford and Warren Forest Service offices. In summer the tape is also available from the campground host at Hearts Content Campground. The name "Hearts Content"

Virgin timber

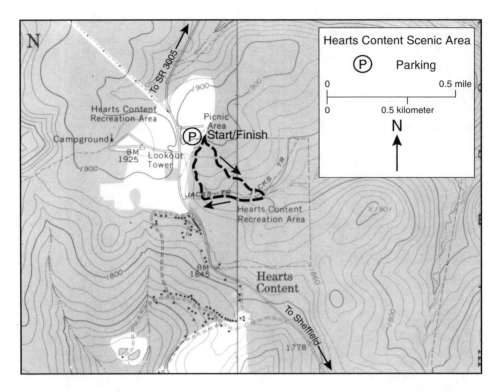

comes from a logging camp of Wheeler and Dusenbury, which in turn copied it from an earlier homestead.

The trailhead for this hike is the Hearts Content picnic area, and the directions for reaching it are the same as for Hickory Creek. The Tom's Run Hike also leaves from the same parking area but now you want the obvious trail that leads to the virgin timber. An interpretive sign at the trailhead illustrates the history of the scenic area.

You come immediately to a marker that proclaims Hearts Content a registered Natural Landmark. The first part of the trail is smooth, compacted limestone for wheelchairs and strollers. Bear right past a dead pine. Many of the white pines are dead or dying, as are many of the beech, which are dying of beech bark disease complex. In the parlance of foresters, the stand is "over

mature," and we are watching the pines being replaced by shade-tolerant hemlocks. Already many of these hemlocks are very large trees in their own right. If left to itself, this forest would become a mixture of hemlock, birch, and red maple.

Soon you reach a small fenced-in area. This is a deer exclosure area, and it's intended to keep our overabundant deer herd from browsing here. You can see a great many more plants, shrubs, and small trees growing within the fence than outside where the deer can eat them. These differences are now profound.

The wheelchair path turns right at this point. Continue on the well-defined gravel path. At 0.6 km (0.4 mile) you reach a memorial to the Wheelers and Dusenburys, who ran their logging business for over a century. Immediately behind the memorial are several springs that constitute the source of the West Branch of Tionesta Creek. All about you are large white pines.

Many companies cut pines this size and sawed them into standard-sized timbers, and boards. Wheeler and Dusenbury specialized in long timbers. Their mill at Endeavor could cut logs up to 30 meters (100 feet) long. These long logs were primarily used as bridge timbers, but earlier in the century they had been used for masts and spars on sailing ships. Such logs could not be loaded onto a single log car. Unless two steam-powered log loaders were available, they had to be loaded by hand. Wheeler and Dusenbury were still supplying such special timbers when most of the rest of Penn's Woods had been cut over.

Beyond the memorial, you cross the headwaters of the West Branch and head back upstream. Other trees growing here are red maple, yellow birch, black birch, black cherry and white ash. At 1.3 km (0.8 mile) you turn right again, and at 1.7 km (1.1 miles), after passing another deer exclosure, you reach another junction with the wheelchair accessible trail. Continue on the compacted limestone surface, and you will soon be back at the parking lot.

From the parking lot walk north to a shelter housing a white pine timber squared by hand. Before railroads and steam-powered sawmills were built in all corners of the state, the only way to get timber to market was to raft it down the rivers leading to the Allegheny and Ohio. In those days, timbers were squared by hand and rafted as far as Cincinnati, Ohio, and Louisville, Kentucky.

19

Anders Natural Area

Distance: 3.2 km (2.0 miles)

Time: 1½ hours

Rise: 58 meters (190 feet)

Highlight: Old-growth white pines

Map: USGS 7½' Youngsville

Just west of Warren, near the town of Irvine, lies a small tract of old-growth white pine along Anders Run. The Western Pennsylvania Conservancy, with help from the Northern Allegheny Conservation Association, the DeFrees Family Foundation, and the National Forge Company, bought this tract and subsequently transferred the 39 hectares (nearly 100 acres) to Cornplanter State Forest.

The Anders Tract is conveniently close to the Allegheny River and must have been cut very early in the 19th century. The old-growth white pine and hemlock are estimated to be 180 years old. The largest pines are more than a meter in diameter and up to 36 meters tall. Climax vegetation in this part of Penn's Woods is probably a mixture of hemlock and northern hardwoods such as beech. At Cook Forest State Park and Hearts Content Scenic Area you can see that the old white pine are dying, and the climax forest is taking over. The Anders Tract is relatively young, and its pines should be with us for a couple of centuries to come.

To reach the trailhead from US 6 west of Warren, turn south on US 62, and in just 0.2 mile turn right for Buckaloons Recreation Area on SR 3022. Continue past Buckaloons and the Northeast Forest Experiment Station. After 0.9 mile, turn left on the paved Dunns Eddy River Road. Drive south for 1.0 mile, and park in the large area on the left side of the road. Foot bridges have been built across Anders Run, so you can manage this hike with walking shoes. No horse or

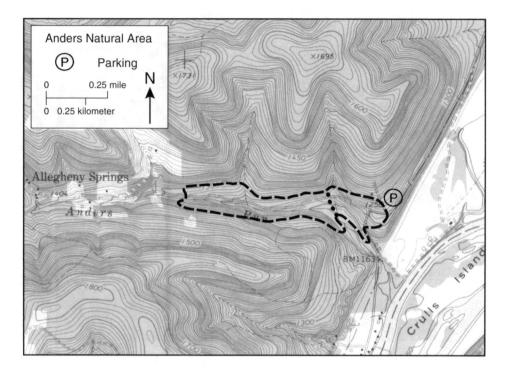

bike riding is permitted at Anders Natural Area. The trail system has been changed so that it is no longer necessary to retrace any of your steps.

To start the hike, follow the yellow plastic squares and older yellow paint blazes down an old route of the Dunns Eddy River Road. Pass some of the big white pines, and at 200 meters (650 feet) turn left on the paved road. Be careful as this section is on a curve and there is a surprising amount of traffic. At 0.4 km (0.2 mile) turn right on trail. The best wildflowers are found here, including red and white trilliums.

Cross a run on rocks to reach a trail junction at 0.7 km (0.4 miles). The red-blazed short loop comes in from the right but turn left and cross Anders Run on a footbridge. Continue downstream before bearing right and climbing gently to the edge of Anders Run Valley. The trail is well supplied with benches and there is one at the top of the climb. Cross several dry water courses. Most of the big trees up here are hemlocks, and Anders Run can frequently be seen. Continue upstream at the top of the slope.

At 1.7 km (1.1 miles) switchback down to Anders Run, and cross it on a footbridge. Traverse the gravel road, climb some steps, and continue among more large white pines. Climb to an old road and turn right at 2.0 km (1.2 miles). Next cross a stream on a culvert and turn right on trail. Go over several side streams on bridges, and then follow a relocation around a great red oak that has fallen across the trail. Other trees growing at Anders are white oak, beech, hemlock, and ash.

Pass the junction with the red-blazed cutoff trail at 2.7 km (1.7 miles). Cross a couple more streams on bog bridges. Climb

Trillium

some steps, and continue past a last bench to the paved road across from the parking lot. Cross with care.

Other hiking opportunities near the Anders Tract are Hearts Content Scenic Area (Hike 18), Tom's Run (Hike 22), Hickory Creek Trail (Hike 32), and Chapman State Park (Hike 29).

20

Beaver Meadows

Distance: 5.8 km (3.6 miles)

Time: 2½ hours

Rise: 70 meters (220 feet)

Highlights: Lake; shadbush; evergreens; blueberries

Maps: USGS 7½' Lynch, USFS Brochure

Beaver Meadows Recreation Area consists of a forest service campground, a lake, and a hiking trail system north of Marienville in Allegheny National Forest. The recreation area can be reached from downtown Marienville on PA 66 by turning north on Forest Road 128. There is a RECREATION AREA sign at the intersection. After 3.8 miles turn right on Forest Road 282. It's another 0.9 mile to a parking area on the right just beyond the dam.

The terrain is fairly flat, making this hike suitable for children, but look out for mountain bikes, which are also allowed on the trail.

To start your hike, walk back to the dam, and cross it to a trail junction. Avoid Salmon Creek Loop, and turn left on Beaver Meadows Loop, marked with white plastic diamonds. The trail passes through scattered stands of red pine and spruce. At 0.9 km (0.6 mile) turn left on the Lakeside Loop marked with blue diamonds. After viewing the lake, return to the main trail and turn left.

Continue ahead at 1.4 km (0.9 mile) where the Penoke Path diverges to the right. Note how the signpost is shielded with aluminum to protect it from porcupines. Next, pass some small blueberry plantings, which have been fenced off to keep them from being eaten by deer.

At 1.9 km (1.2 miles) the Penoke Path comes in from the right on an old logging railroad grade. This appears to have been operated by Central Pennsylvania Lumber of Sheffield. Continue ahead on a floating boardwalk over Penoke Run and the flanking wetlands. In season the far side of

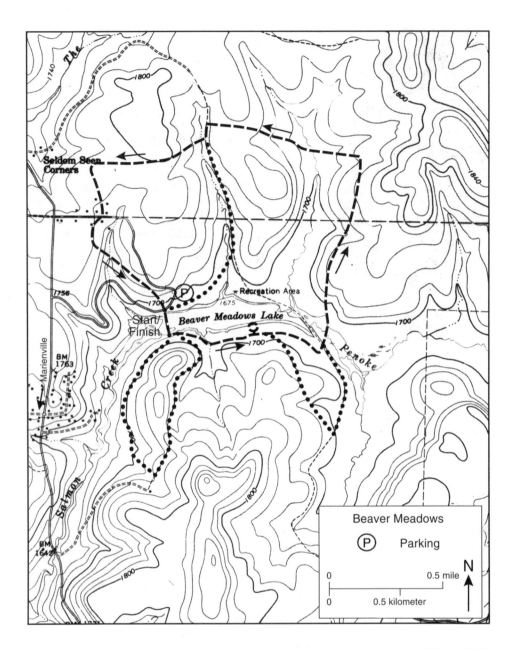

Penoke Run is lined with a phalanx of shadbush. The trail now enters hardwoods, including black cherry, beech, and, of course, red maple. At least 29 percent of the trees in Allegheny National Forest are red maple. Cross a stream at 2.9 km (1.8 miles) as best you can. Note white and red pines growing here.

Cross a bridge over a run at 3.2 km (2.0 miles). Turn left on the old CPL logging

Beaver Meadows Recreation Area

railroad grade. Then turn right at 4.0 km (2.5 miles) on Seldom Seen Trail marked with blue diamonds. Cross a stream on stepping stones, and pass by a forest of plastic tubes. The tops of the tubes are covered with netting to keep birds from getting caught in them. Seedlings must be planted in these tubes to protect them from deer. Trees most likely to be planted in the plastic tubes are black cherry, red oak, and tulip poplar. When Pennsylvania was logged off at the turn of the 19th century, deer had been extirpated. Had deer been present, the forests we see today would not have come back. Pennsylvania might well be covered with ferns, mountain laurel, and grass. Deer were later reintroduced by the Pennsylvania Game Commission.

As you follow the old woods road, stop and listen to the wind song in the pines above. Then turn right on the trail and you soon reach a large blueberry planting. Again, the plants must be protected from deer. Enjoy the blueberries in late July and early August when the gate will be left unlocked. In April 1990 some 550 highbush blueberries were planted. Not all have survived. Earlier in the season look for mayapples.

Follow the old road carefully as there are few markers until you reenter the woods. Next, pass a gate and turn right on trail at the edge of the campground, passing a working water pump. Continue on trail to 5.6 km (3.5 miles) where you turn left on the road, and return to your car.

This hike could be truncated by following the Beaver Meadows Loop along the logging railroad to the parking lot. It could be extended by taking the Salmon Creek Loop (add 2.1 km/1.3 miles) and the Penoke Path (add 1.3 km/0.8 miles).

21

Browns Run

Distance: 6.0 km (3.7 miles)

Time: 2 hours

Rise: 90 meters (300 feet)

Highlights: Evergreens; North Country Trail

Maps: USGS 7½' Cooksburg; state park map; Baker Trail maps

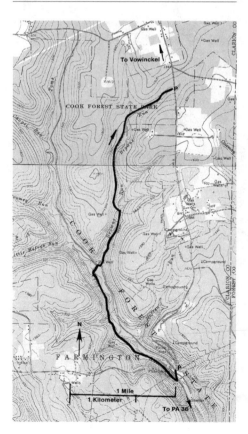

This is an easy hike in the more remote parts of Cook Forest State Park. All the stream crossings are bridged, and the route follows old roads and railroad grades. The trade-off is that there are no blazes. This trail is almost entirely through a thick growth of hemlocks and white pines. (See Hike 26 for information on the history of Cook Forest State Park.) It also requires a straight-forward car shuttle. This is a very pretty trail with little climbing, and it could be done in the opposite direction. Walking shoes should be fine for this hike.

Cook Forest State Park is on PA 36 about 15 miles north of exit 78 on I-80 at Brookville. Both trailheads are on the Vowinckel Road. The first is 4.0 miles north of PA 36 or 1.8 miles south of PA 66 at Vowinckel. Leave one car at a small area on the east side of the road. Then drive south for 3.0 miles on the Vowinckel Road, and park at the Log Cabin Inn Nature Center, which is the same trailhead used for Hike 26.

To start the hike, head across the stone bridge over Toms Run, and turn right on the combined Liggett and Baker Trails. These trails follow the grade of the logging railroad that supplied the sawmill at Cooksburg for so many years. The North Country Trail logo shows that the Baker Trail has been designated as part of this great but unfinished national scenic trail. However since nearly 2 km (some 1.3 miles) of this hike are on a bridle path, it can never be certified by the National Park Service.

Soon you pass a signed junction with the Camp Trail, which leads uphill left to the Ridge Campground. At 0.5 km (0.3 mile)

North Country National Scenic Trail

you cross a wooden bridge that is typical of the care with which the cross streams have been bridged on this trail.

Keep right on the Baker Trail at 0.8 km (0.5 mile) where the Corduroy Trail diverges to the left. You cross three more bridges of pressure-treated lumber before reaching 1.7 km (1.1 miles) where the Liggett Trail turns right and traverses Toms Run on a commercial steel bridge. Continue ahead on the Baker and Brown Run Trails.

At 2.3 km (1.4 miles) turn right off the old railroad grade and cross a steel bridge over Toms Run. Then jog right on the unpaved Toms Run road for 30 meters (100 feet) and continue on an old road that makes a green tunnel through the evergreens. At 3.0 km (1.9 miles) you get your first look at Browns Run itself. Turn left at 3.5 km (2.2 miles) where the Deer Meadow Trail goes right, and cross a bridge over Browns Run. Then turn right on the Bridle Trail. Yes, this trail is designated for horses, but considering how close the stables are on the Vowinckel Road, there is little evidence of such usage. The trail continues through evergreens galore with occasional glimpses of Browns Run.

At 5.0 km (3.1 miles) bear left off the old railroad grade, and follow some blue-plastic markers across a bridge. Soon you return to the same old railroad grade, still following the blue markers. Keep right on the Baker and Browns Run Trails at 5.3 km (3.3 miles) where the Bridle Trail diverges to the left. Next you cross a couple of plank bridges, and arrive at the paved Vowinckel Road. Turn left to reach the parking area and your car.

There is additional hiking of the in-and-out variety ahead on the Baker Trail, which crosses Greenwood Road and continues through virgin timber before reaching the park boundary. See the park map.

22

Tom's Run

Distance: 6.4 km (4.0 miles)

Time: 2 hours

Rise: 120 meters (400 feet)

Highlights: Mountain stream; Tanbark Trail; logging railroad grades

Maps: USGS 7½' Cherry Grove, Cobham

Within Allegheny National Forest the Tanbark Trail, which once stretched from Tionesta Scenic Area to US 62, used to be second in length only to the North Country Trail. The original, or southern, route of the North Country Trail crossed some private land within Allegheny National Forest. When the owners began to have second thoughts about the North Country Trail, the U.S. Forest Service simply abandoned the original route. The North Country Trail was relocated on the Tanbark Trail, reducing the Tanbark Trail to a 14 kilometer (8.7 mile) section from near Dunham Siding to US 62. Nevertheless, the Tanbark passes through or near some of the most beautiful parts of Allegheny National Forest.

This hike uses part of the Tanbark Trail near Hearts Content Scenic Area and old logging railroad grades of Wheeler and Dusenbury that have been cleared as cross-country ski trails to make a loop through the valley of Tom's Run and the uppermost part of the West Branch of Tionesta Creek. Ordinary walking shoes should do for this hike because the crossings of Tom's Run have been eliminated.

The trailhead is the picnic area at Hearts Content Scenic Area. If space permits, you can park in the picnic area lot, which has some shade around the edges, or use the large lot next door for the Hickory Creek Trail. Avoid the obvious trail that leads to the virgin timber. Instead, follow a trail to the left that's marked with blue-plastic diamonds nailed to the trees. The cross-country ski trail parallels the northern boundary of the Hearts Content Scenic Area and descends gently.

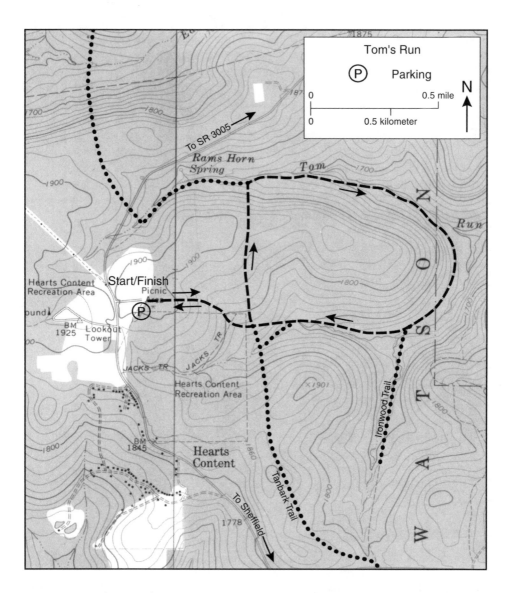

At 0.8 km (0.5 mile) turn left on the Tanbark Trail, which is marked with white-plastic diamonds. Follow the Tanbark over a low ridge and down the north slope. At the bottom of the hill at 1.8 km (1.1 miles) turn right on Tom's Run Trail which is again marked with blue diamonds. The trail is a logging railroad grade, and you follow it across a small meadow. You can recognize that you're following an old railroad grade by the parallel depressions that cross the grade where the ties rotted in place. Indeed, in some wet places you can actually see the old ties themselves. They weren't squared or creosoted; they were just lengths of locally grown trees.

At some spots the grade tunnels through the hemlocks and at others it crosses open meadows. At one point in a meadow a family of grouse was flushed, the chicks heading off in one direction, the hen in the other. The hen circled back, displaying her "broken wing" and cheeping piteously as she tried to draw me away from her chicks. Soon the wing healed miraculously, and she circled around me to collect her brood.

At 3.0 km (1.9 miles) bear right on a relocation which avoids a pair of crossings of Tom's Run. At 3.3 km (2.1 miles) you pass the white-blazed boundary of State Game Land No. 29. Stick to the old railroad grade, and begin the gentle climb back to the plateau. What a joy it would be to ski these trails! Your first sight of the West Branch near 4.3 km (2.7 miles) confirms that you are now walking upstream.

By the time you reach a junction with a blue-blazed ski trail at 4.6 km (2.9 miles) you have recrossed onto national forest land. Keep right on Tom's Run Trail, avoiding the Ironwood Trail that crosses the stream. Follow Tom's Run Trail back to the crossing of the Tanbark Trail. Then continue ahead, retracing your steps to the parking lot at Hearts Content.

This hike could be extended by following the Ironwood Trail out to Hearts Content Road and returning on the Tanbark trail.

23

Buzzard Swamp

Distance: 8.2 km (5.1 miles)

Time: 2¾ hours

Rise: 20 meters (60 feet)

Highlights: Ponds; birds

Maps: USGS 7½' Marienville East, USFS Brochure

The Buzzard Swamp system of interconnecting trails consists of a number of forestry roads that have been gated off. Over 17 kilometers (10 miles) of trails traverse a region with little local relief, managed jointly by the U.S. Forest Service and Pennsylvania Game Commission as a wildlife viewing and hiking area. Earth dams have been built, producing 15 ponds of various sizes plus many more small puddles. The wildlife viewing is the best in Allegheny National Forest. Mountain bikes are permitted but the old roads are wide and flat, so there should be ample room for everyone on the trails.

Buzzard Swamp is located southeast of Marienville. This hike is written as a car shuttle, but several circuits are possible from the western trailhead. From Seven Points in downtown Marienville, drive south on the paved Loleta Road (SR 2005). There is a RECREATION AREA sign but it probably refers to Loleta Camp and Picnic Area, not to Buzzard Swamp. At 1.3 miles turn left on Forestry Road 157. Note a thriving beaver colony along here. A bulldozer has heaped up a berm to keep the beaver pond from flooding across the road. Drive east for 2.3 miles to a large parking area at the trailhead. Leave one car here, and return to Marienville in the other. Turn right on Spruce Street at the Bucktail Hotel at Seven Points, and drive east for 4.4 miles. This is Forest Road 130 according to the map, but I saw no sign. Park at a very obscure area on the right. It is the first opportunity after Forest Road 559 on the left.

Evidence of beavers in Buzzard Swamp

Make sure you have some insect repellent in your pack and take your hat, binoculars and bird book, but you can get by with walking shoes. Dodge around the gate and head down the old forestry road. The road is marked with occasional blue diamonds for cross-country skiing, and at certain spots they will be useful. Note how the brush has been cut back around wild apple trees. Such trees provide food for wildlife, but they can't compete with forest trees. Legend has it such trees were planted by lumberjacks throwing away their apple cores. Apples were the only fruit they got, but they got barrels of them. At one point a serviceberry, or shadbush was given the same treatment as the old apple trees. Serviceberries must provide wildlife with food as well, and with a high water table there may be a good yield. Without lots of water serviceberries taste like a stale Pop Tart, but with water they are the taste that agribusiness forgot.

Meadows have been cleared to the sides of the roads. Bluebird boxes are installed in them, but I didn't see any residents. I checked one box and found it didn't have any bottom.

At 0.7 km (0.4 mile) you come to pond 13. Canada geese nest along many of the ponds. Woodduck boxes have also been installed. The newer boxes appear to be made out of plastic. Red-winged blackbirds are abundant. So are tree swallows, who nest in the boxes near the ponds. One swallow held his ground on top of his box as I approached and allowed me to take his picture before he flew off. A beaver lodge was visible in one of the ponds along Crooked Run.

At 2.0 km (1.2 miles) bear left and cross the dam forming pond 8. Then continue through the woods, passing a large meadow that goes all the way to pond 7. At 3.0 km (1.9 miles) continue ahead. Most of these junctions are marked with a map on a post, and a screw or nail marks your location on the

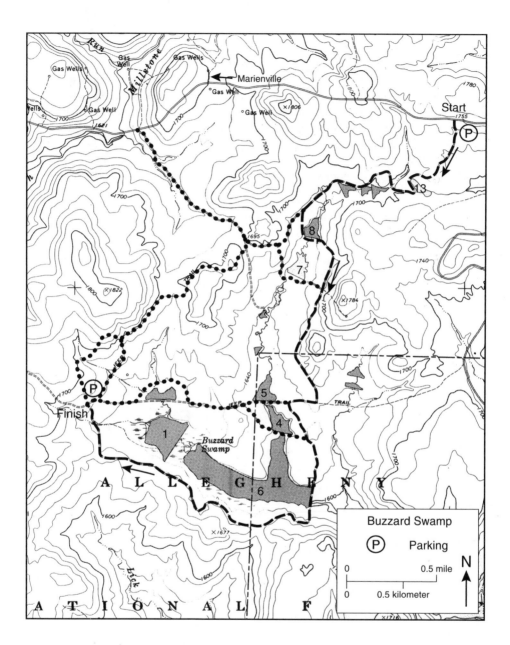

map. Note the effects of porcupine attacks on some of these posts. Even the aluminum sheathing on one post was torn apart.

Ignore a road to the left at 3.9 km (2.4 miles). Then bear right and emerge into a very large open area. Turn left after 4.3 km (2.7 miles). Ponds 4 and 5 are visible ahead. Pass some plots where game foods are grown. Then cross the wide spillway for pond 6, and continue across the dam. Pond 6 is the largest pond at Buzzard Swamp, and you can see far up it from the dam. It's about

1.5 km (0.9 mile) long. At one point there was a well-developed game trail over the dam.

In the woods the road swings west, paralleling the south shore of pond 6. At 6.0 km (3.7 miles) there is a large meadow looking north across pond 6. The corner of the 17-hectare (42-acre) propagation area is reached at 7.1 km (4.4 miles). Entry is prohibited in order to permit waterfowl to reproduce undisturbed. At 7.2 km (4.5 miles) there is a view of pond 1 in the propagation area. The road then swings right, crossing several culverts that provide the inflow into the ponds on Muddy Fork.

At 8.2 km (5.1 miles) you reach the gate and parking area at the end of Forest Road 157.

Several loops, including the Songbird Sojourn Interpretive Trail, are possible from this trailhead.

24

Clear Creek State Park

Distance: 8.3 km (5.2 miles)

Time: 3½ hours

Rise: 270 meters (880 feet)

Highlights: Evergreen plantations; pileated woodpeckers

Maps: USGS 7½' Sigel; state park map

Clear Creek is a small state park just across the Clarion River from Allegheny National Forest. There are about 24 kilometers (15 miles) of trails in this park of only 485 hectares (1,200 acres). The park occupies the valley of Clear Creek between PA 949 and the Clarion. You'll traverse the camping area in the park, so observe the prohibition on pets in that area. Despite some rocks and a few wet areas, good walking shoes should be adequate.

Clear Creek State Park is on Pa 949, and the trailhead at the beach house parking area is 3.9 miles from the junction with PA 36 in Sigel, which in turn is about 7 miles north of exit 78 on I-80 in Brookville. The hike starts on the Clear Creek Trail which you will find in the far left hand corner of the parking lot. This trail is marked with white diamond-shaped blazes.

To start, bear left almost immediately and climb. Continue through a Norway spruce plantation with occasional aspen volunteers. Witch hazel is also found along the trail, and at one place you pass a serviceberry that has grown to the size of a small tree.

Soon you cross the Phyllis Run Trail, and shortly after that the Ridge Trail diverges to the left. The trail then passes through a rhododendron thicket. Note the association between this shrub and the many spring seeps. Next, you pass the Big Coon Trail which descends toward Clear Creek. Black cherry is found along this section of the trail, and at another spot you see a large sandstone boulder on its leisurely slide to the creek below.

Clear Creek Trail

This crow-sized bird is the largest woodpecker in the world next to the extraordinarily rare ivory-billed woodpecker. Its presence is usually revealed by large oval holes chiseled up to eight inches deep into trees. Its flight is swooping and reveals large white underwing patches. The call is like that of a flicker but louder, deeper, and woodier. Surprisingly, the holes it makes in search of ants and grubs don't kill the trees, and in fact its radical surgery may actually save the tree from these parasites.

At 2.0 km (1.2 miles) keep left at a junction with the Oxshoe Trail that diverges to the right, and at 2.4 km (1.5 miles) bear right on the paved road in the campground. In traversing the campground, you pass drinking water and cross Clear Creek on the road bridge. The Clarion River is on your left, and some benches are provided for enjoying the view. At 2.9 km (1.9 miles) turn left on a paved road. Soon the Pipeline Trail, which can be used to shorten this hike, diverges to the right. Keep right where the road splits. The park's exercise trail is just to your left.

Bear right to the River Trail at 3.6 km (2.3 miles) and shortly turn right on the Hunter Trail. You now begin the only real climb on this hike.

The Hunter Trail is marked mostly with large irregularly shaped white blazes that have been painted over with pink at some time. This trail would be a real challenge to your pathfinding skills, but fortunately it's quite straight. There are also a few metal trail markers. In hunting season there are signs proclaiming that hunting, shooting, trapping, and dog training are prohibited in the no-hunting portion of the park to your right. These signs are tied on with string and might be removed when hunting season is over.

The top of the hill is reached at 4.3 km (2.7 miles), and shortly the trail turns right. It

At 1.3 km (0.8 mile) you arrive at the top of a steep bank above the creek, adorned with a white pine, and soon you turn left on an old railroad grade. This may be the old Frazier Railroad, which served two steam-powered sawmillls farther up the Clear Creek valley in the 1860s. It isn't known whether the Frazier Railroad even had a locomotive; it could have used horses. There was no connecting railroad along the Clarion at that time, so the lumber must have been floated downstream on rafts or flatboats.

Immediately beyond, you cross the pipeline swath that cuts across the valley. Note the apple trees growing inside a fence to protect them from deer. Then you pass a walk-in picnic area, and at 1.5 km (0.9 mile) you cross Truby Run on a steel bridge and continue on the old tram road. The Sawmill Trail comes in from the left at 1.7 km (1.1 miles).

One of the largest birds you might see in these woods is the pileated woodpecker.

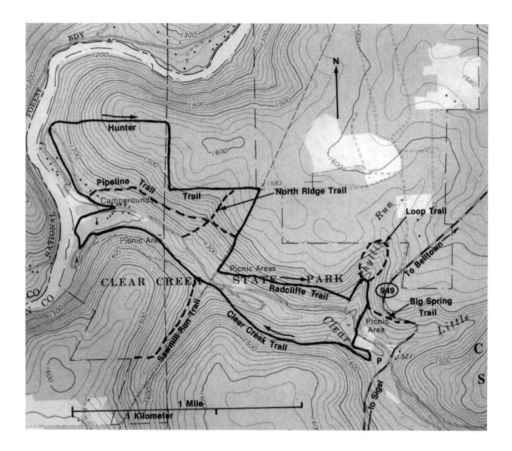

continues in this new direction until it reaches the edge of Clear Creek Valley. After starting to descend, it turns sharply left, regains the hilltop, and continues past a junction with the North Ridge Trail at 5.7 km (3.6 miles). Turn right on the pipeline, and note the larch trees planted here to soften the visual impact of the swath. This swath is a good place to see deer.

A large boulder at 6.0 km (3.7 miles) provides a view across the valley. Soon the Pipeline Trail joins from the right, and you turn left on the Radcliffe Trail at 6.3 km (3.9 miles). The Radcliffe Trail is reached near the bottom of the hill, just before the large valves on the gas pipeline. The Radcliffe Trail is marked with yellow diamonds and

proceeds through a plantation of white pine and Norway spruce. Where the trail meets some red pines, it moves farther up the hillside.

At 7.4 km (4.6 miles) turn left on the Phyllis Run Trail in the midst of another spruce plantation. Phyllis Run Trail is marked with red blazes painted in the shape of a girl with big hair. Pass an unsafe piped spring, and then bypass the longer loop, cross Phyllis Run, and head back down the other side. Shortly the Big Spring Trail diverges left, and at 7.9 km (4.9 miles) you turn left on the paved park road. Keep right, and in only 50 meters (55 yards) find a flight of steps leading down to several picnic shelters. Cut through the picnic area to the dam, and use the footbridge to cross. A plaque says the dam was built by the Civilian Conservation Corps in 1934.

Beyond the dam, turn left and pass between the beach and beach house to the gated access road. You are back at the beach house parking lot and your car.

This hike uses only four of the 17 trails in Clear Creek State Park. There is plenty of additional hiking here and across PA 949 in Clear Creek State Forest on the Beartown Rocks (Hike 25) and Clear Creek Trails.

25

Beartown Rocks

Distance: 9.5 km (5.9 miles)

Time: 3¾ hours

Rise: 165 meters (540 feet)

Highlights: View; black forest

Maps: USGS 7½' Sigel; Clear Creek
State Forest Hiking Trails

This delightful hike follows Clear Creek and Trap Run in Clear Creek State Forest to a view across the Clarion into Allegheny National Forest. Beartown Rocks is an interpretive trail, and along the way you will learn all about the area—from the logging era to the petroleum age to the Civilian Conservation Corps of the Great Depression to contemporary forestry practice. The area was burned in the Sigel fire of 1906, so most of the trees are of the same age. So powerful was this fire that it jumped the Clarion River and burned well into what is now Allegheny National Forest before burning itself out.

The trailhead for this hike is the beach parking area for Clear Creek State Park on PA 949, which is 3.9 miles from Sigel. This is the same trailhead as Hike 24 (Clear Creek State Park). Hiking boots are recommended for this hike.

To start, cross PA 949, and find the orange-blazed Beartown Rocks Trail at the end of the highway guide rail. Immediately you enter a black forest of Norway spruce planted by the Civilian Conservation Corps (CCC). All these trees were planted the same day, but look at the difference in sizes. Those planted along the creek are much larger than those planted farther back.

The CCC was a product of the first hundred days of Franklin Roosevelt's administration. Roosevelt was inaugurated in March, and the first CCC camps were opened in June. Such was the speed with which the CCC and other agencies were cobbled together that spring that army officers were placed in charge of the

camps; after all, they didn't have anything else to do.

A member of the CCC was paid $30 per month, and $25 went back to his family, leaving $5 for the recruit. Weekly entertainment consisted of a bath in the creek followed by a trip into Brookville. Even in winter the recruits lived in tents. By 1941, three million young men had served in the CCC, eating three square meals a day, growing stronger and healthier, and helping their families. They built recreational facilities still used today as well as roads and trails, and they planted millions of trees. Over 85 percent of them served in World War II.

The trail follows along Clear Creek. At 0.6 km (0.4 mile) cross a pole line and bridge. Soon you begin to cross steel pipes on the ground. These are relics of a small oil field that was pumped dry.

Next, cross a bridge over Clear Creek, and pass through a meadow. Many oil wells were pumped by a natural gas engine at this site. The power was transmitted to the individual wells by means of steel rods. You can see a working system at the Drake Well Museum south of Titusville.

Bear right in the meadow, and recross Clear Creek. Note steel tripods in the woods along the trail. These tripods held the rods that pumped the various wells in the field. When production fell to a few liters per day the field was abandoned.

Recross Clear Creek and continue upstream, passing the ruins of a dam used for logging in 1870. Water was stored by the dam and then released to float logs down stream. At 1.5 km (0.9 mile) avoid a bridge to the left. Shortly, turn right on Trap Run Loop, and climb on an old road. This road forms the boundary between stands of evergreens on the left and more open deciduous woods on the right. Continue ahead at a junction. Hemlocks add to the collection of evergreens, and at times the trail is a tunnel through the rho-

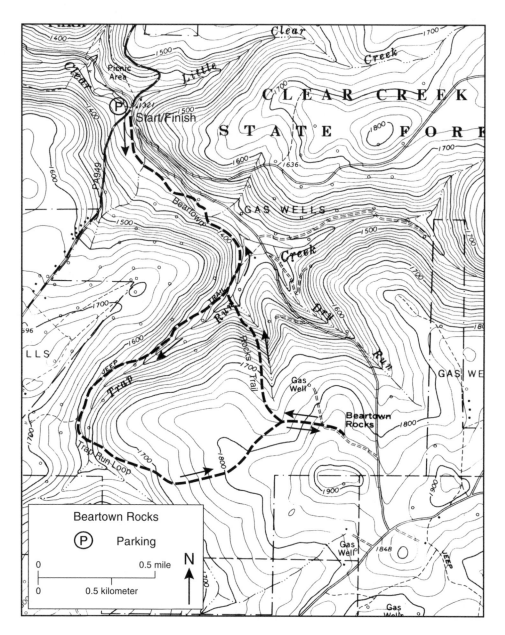

dodendrons. At 2.9 km (1.8 miles) pass a side trail to Campers Paradise, which is a commercial campground on PA 949. Much of the understory here consists of small white pines.

Next, bear left and cross Trap Run at 3.3 km (2.1 miles). The bridge is decked with old oil pipes. Then turn right at the gas well and continue on a rough narrow trail through mountain laurel. Follow blazes carefully as the trail continues upstream along Trap Run.

At 4.1 km (2.5 miles) the trail emerges into more open woods and then picks up an old woods road. Turn left at 5.1 km (3.2 miles) onto another woods road. There's a gas pipeline installation at this corner. Pass a gas well on the right before reaching a critical turn at 5.3 km (3.3 miles). You turn off the woods road onto trail. This turn really ought to be double-blazed. Inadvertent double blazes seen elsewhere along the trail do not denote turns but suggest that blazing and reblazing were done by people of different vertical attainment.

Turn right on Beartown Rocks Trail at 5.8 km (3.6 miles). Then cross one woods road and continue on another. Finally, turn left on trail, and reach the parking lot at Beartown Rocks. Yes, you could have driven here, but think of all you would have missed along the way.

The eponymous rocks are house-sized blocks of Pottsville sandstone that have weathered along joint cracks. Who would live in a town out in the woods but bears?

Climb the steps to the highest rock for a view to the north. Note how flat the Allegheny Plateau really is.

Retrace your steps to the junction of the Beartown Rocks and Trap Run Trails. Continue ahead on the Beartown Rocks Trail and cross an intermittent stream. Then descend steeply on a log skid. Such skids were used to move logs down hill. Steep ones like this worked on gravity and a little ice, while on shallower skids horses had to pull the logs along the slide. Cross a bridge at 7.6 km (4.7 miles) and reach a trail box where you can register.

Next pass a gas well, and cross Trap Run on a bridge to reach the junction with the other end of the Trap Run Loop Trail. Continue ahead on Beartown Rocks Trail, and retrace your steps to the parking lot on PA 949.

Other nearby hiking opportunities are Clear Creek Trail on this side of PA 949 and Clear Creek State Park on the other side of the highway.

26

Cook Forest State Park

Distance: 10.2 km (6.3 miles)

Time: 4 hours

Rise: 370 meters (1,220 feet)

Highlights: Virgin timber; lookout tower

Maps: USGS 7½' Cooksburg; state park map; Baker Trail maps

Logging started early in what is now Cook Forest State Park. John Cook began cutting along Toms Run in 1828. Rafts made of squared white pine logs were floated to Pittsburgh. This business was continued by Cook's son Anthony, then in turn by the grandchildren. A small patch of timber, only a short distance from the sawmill on Toms Run, had been left standing with the intention that it be cut just before the sawmill was dismantled. In the 1920s, the Cook Forest Association raised $200,000, and with $450,000 from the state they used it to purchase Cook Forest State Park. Thus one of the largest stands of virgin white pine was saved from the ax. At other locations in the park virgin hemlock is found. But what man has saved, nature may still destroy. Violent windstorms, one in 1956 and another in 1976, devastated different parts of the forest, felling rows of trees. The park has also been damaged by floods. In June 1981 one flood washed out several footbridges across Toms Run, severing the Baker and other trails. This hike visits several areas of virgin timber, Cook Forest fire tower, and a lookout over the Clarion River, using parts of the Baker and other trails.

Cook Forest State Park is on PA 36, about 15 miles north of exit 78 on I-80 at Brookville. This hike starts from the Log Cabin Inn Visitor Center on Vowinckel Road, 1 mile north of the junction with PA 36 in Cooksburg. There is abundant parking space and rest rooms are available at the adjacent picnic area. There are wet areas along this hike, but the footway is generally

Clarion River

good, so you should be able to do the hike with ordinary walking shoes.

To start the hike, turn left on the paved Vowinkel Road, facing traffic, and cross the stone bridge over Toms Run. Pass the Liggett-Baker Trail (see Hike 21), and continue to shelter no. 1, where you cross the road and head up the Ridge Trail. Trails in Cook Forest are marked with signs at intersections but are not blazed in between. Usually they are easy to follow but when the ground is covered with freshly fallen leaves the trails can test your pathfinding skills. The climb passes among large hemlocks, and you reach the top of the hill at 0.9 km (0.5 mile). At the end of the Ridge Trail in the campground, turn left on the paved road, and follow it out to PA 36 at 1.6 km (1.0 mile).

Cross the highway, and bear right on the exit from the one-way road to the lookout tower. Where the exit road splits, keep right on the part that heads back to the highway.

At the point where you return to PA 36, find the Mohawk Trail and turn left. Immediately you are in a beautiful stand of virgin hemlocks interspersed with a few white pines and giant beeches. At 2.9 km (1.8 miles) turn right on Tower Road. At the top of a rise look carefully for the River Trail crossing (the sign faces the other way), and turn right on this trail at 3.5 km (2.2 miles). The River Trail descends to the Clarion. Several large stands of rhododendron grow along this part of the River Trail as does a patch of mountain laurel. Near the Clarion the River Trail is marked with large but faded white blazes that face across the trail.

At the bottom of the hill the Baker Trail comes in from the right past a natural gas well. The Baker Trail is not blazed through the park, but to the right you can see its yellow markings on the adjacent game land. Take a good look at the Clarion River, down which you can see Hemlock Island, and then turn left (upstream), still on the River Trail.

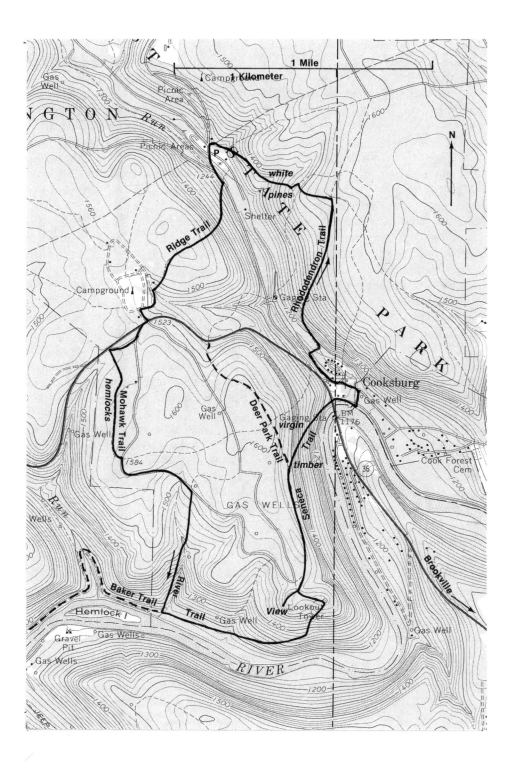

There is more rhododendron along the river.

At 4.8 km (3.0 miles) you cross a meadow and then a side stream. Turn left, and then bear right on an old road grade that draws away from the river and climbs back up the hill. The climb continues to the base of Cook Forest lookout tower. Near the top the River Trail switchbacks back and forth, but your way is complicated by a number of herd paths that cut off the switchbacks. Avoid the herd paths, and do your best to follow the large faded white blazes. The best views from the tower are north up Toms Run and east up the Clarion.

Back on the ground, follow the heavily used trail to the Seneca Trail junction, and turn left to Seneca Point, which is a natural vista down the Clarion River. Then backtrack on the Seneca Trail, and continue past the rest rooms and parking area along the edge of the hill. At 6.8 km (4.2 miles) the Deer Park Trail diverges to the left, and you start down the side of the hill on the Seneca Trail through another stand of virgin hemlock and white pine. Soon you enter the area damaged by the tornado of July 11, 1976. The trail has been reestablished, so it's easy to follow, and there's a view of the Clarion below. Soon you reenter the woods where the trail is dug into the steep hillside and continue to the bottom of the slope.

At 7.6 km (4.7 miles) cross PA 36 with care, and continue on the River Road, passing the park office. Turn left on the paved road, and circle around an enclave of private land, passing the children's fishing pond and the Indian Cabins. Turn right on the Birch and Rhododendron Trail just before you reach PA 36. Turn right at 8.2 km (5.1 miles), and cross the swinging bridge over Toms Run. At the far side turn right and then left to pick up the Rhododendron Trail, which has already started its climb up the hill. Turn left on the Rhododendron Trail and climb gently on its fine old grade. At 9.1 km (5.7 miles) turn left on the Joyce Kilmer Trail, and then shortly turn left again at a junction with the Indian Trail. At the next junction continue ahead on the Longfellow and Baker Trail, which you follow down the hill.

This is the heart of the forest cathedral. The 60-meter (200-foot) white pines you find here are truly awesome. An ordinary white pine would top out where the first branches on these monarchs begin. Were all Penn's Woods like this from the lake to the sea only 200 years ago? Considering all the demands on forests today—not only timber and pulp but firewood, biomass, and even a new resource base for the chemical industry—can any forest on this planet ever be left long enough to grow trees like these again?

Continue down the Longfellow Trail, or wander up and down the lettered side trails (see the inset on the park map) as the spirit moves you. At 10.1 km (6.3 miles) on the Longfellow Trail you pass the memorial fountain and shortly emerge at the Log Cabin Inn Visitor Center. Stop in to see the exhibits on display before returning to your car.

This hike has used only a quarter of the 43 kilometers (27 miles) of hiking trails in Cook Forest State Park, so there are many additional hiking opportunities. The CCC Trail, just north of the visitor center, is one. See also Hike 21, which leads you into the more remote regions of the park along Browns Run.

27

Minister Creek Trail

Distance: 10.2 km (6.3 miles)

Time: 4½ hours

Rise: 315 meters (1,030 feet)

Highlights: View; cliffs; mountain stream

Maps: USGS 7½' Mayburg, Cherry Grove; Hiker's Guide to Allegheny National Forest, map 7.

Minister Creek is probably the most famous of all the foot trails in Allegheny National Forest—and justly so. It has cliffs, big rocks, beautiful streams, part of the North Country National Scenic Trail, as well as a natural overlook across Minister Valley. When sunlight dapples the forest floor on a day in early fall or wildflowers are in bloom on a spring day, this is one of the best trails to hike in all of Penn's Woods. The Minister Creek Trail has long had a reputation for overuse, but on my hikes I found no evidence of this. Indeed, I didn't meet anybody at all—but then, it was a weekday. Minister Creek is shorter than generally advertised, and although there are many exposed roots in the footway, you should be able to negotiate it with good walking shoes. If you elect to backpack this trail, you will, of course, need hiking boots.

The trailhead for Minister Creek Trail is on PA 666 between the villages of Truemans and Porkey, 14.7 miles southwest of Sheffield. The parking area is just across the road from the Minister Creek campground.

Be aware that Minister Creek Trail is open to mountain bikes. Mountain bikes are quiet and fast, and on occasion they run into hikers with painful or even fatal results.

To start the hike, cross PA 666 and bear left. Then turn right, and follow the white plastic diamonds up an old grade. These plastic markings are not vandal resistant, and in many places you'll have to follow the old blue "eye" blazes now faded or painted over with black. The change in marking was probably decreed by some well-intentioned

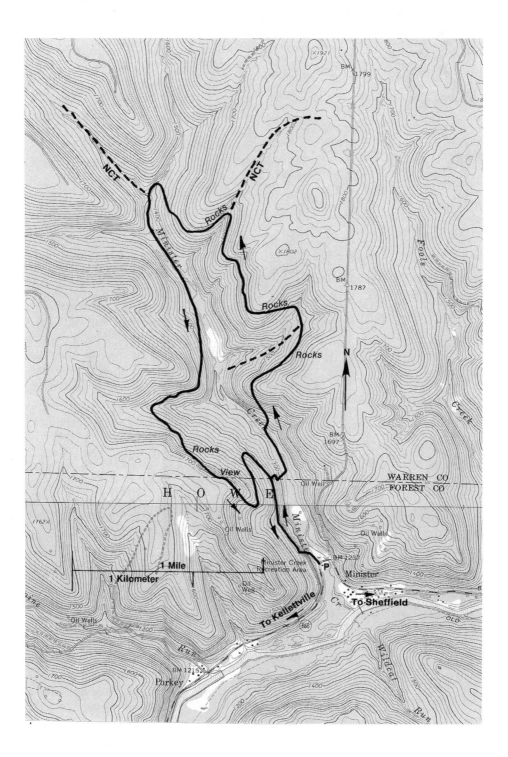

The view across Minister Valley

soul who doesn't hike and has never tried to follow a trail where the plastic diamonds have been torn off and only the sometimes-rusty aluminum nails remain.

Bear right on Forest Road 537 at 0.2 km (0.1 mile). This road is closed to traffic. Note the trees growing on top of a boulder to the right of the trail. Next, avoid a grade to the left, and then pass an old oil well also on the left. Continue ahead on trail at the end of the road and at 0.9 km (0.6 mile) you reach the loop junction. Bear right downhill, passing some large boulders, and turn left on an old logging railroad grade at the bottom of the hill. Next, bear right off the old grade, and cross Minister Creek on a bridge at 1.4 km (0.9 mile).

Beyond the creek the trail climbs gently and is soon out of sight of the creek. Large sandstone boulders can be seen above the trail. At 2.6 km (1.6 miles) a yellow-blazed side trail goes left down a pipeline to Deerlick Camp, about 0.8 km (0.5 mile) from the main trail. A small stream is crossed at 2.8 km (1.7 miles), and then the trail makes its way among more sandstone boulders. Trees along this section are black cherry, birch, maple, and beech. Frequently the footway seems to consist entirely of beech roots.

Another small stream is crossed just before reaching the North Country Trail at 4.2 km (2.6 miles). Turn left on the blue-diamond-marked North Country Trail (some of the blue diamonds have a white circle in the middle) and follow it down the hillside on an old road grade passing a spring.

Note the old apple trees along the trail before you reach Triple Fork Camp at 4.9 km (3.0 miles). Here you cross two of the forks of Minister Creek on log bridges.

Just after the second bridge the North Country Trail turns right, but you continue ahead on the Minister Creek Trail. At 5.4 km (3.3 miles) you cross the third fork on a bridge. Soon the trail follows along the bank of the creek, but at 5.8 km (3.4 miles) it climbs away from the creek before crossing another side stream. Next, you head up a side valley, and at 7.1 km (4.4 miles) you turn sharply left and cross this stream. Beyond, the trail climbs and soon passes among more giant boulders. At 7.7 km (4.8 miles) you reach the base of cliffs of the Pottsville sandstone (note the layers of conglomerate), which are the source of all the giant boulders. Most of the boulders are covered with bright-green moss. The trail continues along the base of the cliffs, passing under overhangs and at one point traversing a narrow cleft behind a detached portion of the cliff. The top of the hill is reached at 8.0 km (5.0 miles) by means of a break in the cliffs. Minister Valley Overlook from the brink of the cliffs is just beyond, from where you can look up and across Minister Valley.

Beyond, the trail descends through a couple of rock shelters. Most of the markers have been removed on this section. Descend on stone steps, and then bear left just before the second rock shelter. Follow the path carefully. Continue to the loop junction at 9.3 km (5.8 miles), and then retrace your steps to your car on PA 666.

Additional hiking opportunities at Minister Creek would depend on following the North Country Trail either to the east or to the west.

28

Brush Hollow Trail

Distance: 10.2 km (6.3 miles)

Time: 3¾ hours

Rise: 160 meters (520 feet)

Highlights: Mountain streams; view

*Maps: USGS 7½' James City;
forestry map*

Brush Hollow Trail is a set of three loop trails just west of Big Mill Creek in the Ridgway District of Allegheny National Forest. Primarily intended for cross-country skiing, the trail is also open to hikers year-round. This hike is a tour around the perimeter of this trail system.

Trails such as this one are in contrast with the old days of cross-country skiing. There were no plowed parking lots then; when you reached the trailhead, you piled out of the car and shoveled a spot to park. Then you put on your wooden skis—either heavy, unbreakable surplus from the 10th Mountain Division with cable bindings, or light and fragile ones with three-pin bindings. If you broke the tip of a wooden ski some distance from the trailhead, you could have real difficulty getting back to the road, so you had to carry a spare ski tip in your pack for emergency repairs.

Since nobody else knew about this trail, your group had to break trail all day. When the person in front of the line became exhausted he or she would pull off to the side and let the next person in line take over, dropping in again at the rear of the line. Today's fiberglass skis are all but unbreakable and usually you will find the trail already tracked.

Be aware that the Brush Hollow Trail System is open to mountain bikes. Mountain bikers should always yield the trail to hikers.

The trailhead is on PA 948, 10.7 miles from the junction with US 219 in Ridgway and about 18 miles from Sheffield. A sign is posted on the highway, and you'll find

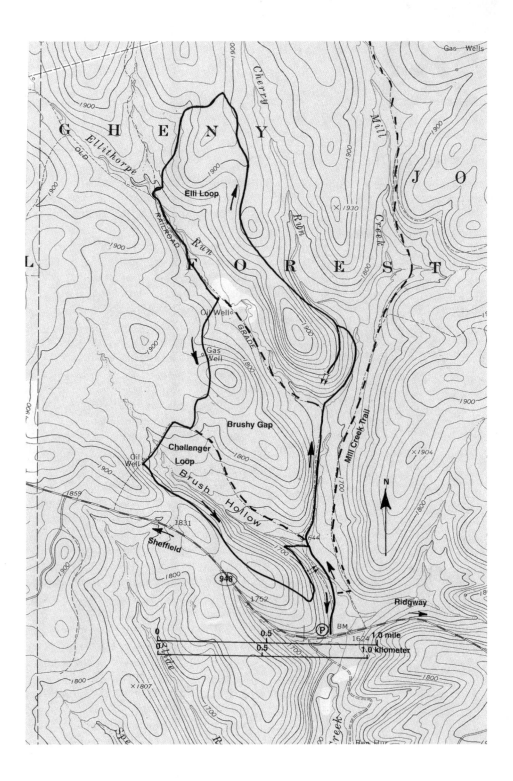

ample parking and an outhouse but no water at the parking lot. Despite some wet spots, walking shoes should be adequate for this hike except in the spring, when you will want your hiking boots. The loop trails permit you to shorten this hike. All the trails are marked with blue-plastic diamonds nailed to trees. Some of these markers have a white arrow on them. The vertical rise is distributed along the hike.

To start your hike, head down the gated old road, and then bear left on an old railroad grade above Mill Creek. At 0.2 km (0.1 mile) you pass a trail to the right marked with white diamonds that connects with the western part of Mill Creek Trail. There are repeated views of Mill Creek and its surrounding hemlocks.

Next, you reach a major trail junction at 0.7 km (0.4 mile). Both ends of the Challenger Loop come in from the left. This is Brush Hollow itself. Note the bridge over the run. There are no steps up or down, so you can ski right across it. All the bridges on the Brush Hollow Trail have been built to this standard. Note springs along the hillside.

Continue ahead up Mill Creek. This valley was first logged by the firm of Hyde and Thayer, which had a sawmill downstream near the Clarion River and used a series of three splash dams to float their logs down Mill Creek.

At the next junction, cross Ellithorpe Run and continue upstream. Beech, yellow birch, and hemlock grow along the creek. In winter look for tracks of deer, wild turkey, and squirrel in the snow. Deer tracks show their cloven hooves. Turkey tracks look like those of a fossil dinosaur. Squirrel tracks have smaller front than hind hocks and start or end near the base of a tree.

Next, the trail tunnels through a spruce plantation. It then swings left and starts to climb the hill above Cherry Run, leaving the railroad grade behind. Logging railroads along Big Mill Creek were first built by Henry, Bayard and Company about 1897. After the saw timber was all cut, the track was pulled up. It was relaid in 1905 by the New York and Pennsylvania Company for their paper mill in Johnsonburg. The New York and Pennsylvania, which cut the small hemlocks and hardwoods for pulp, was the only paper company in Pennsylvania to use a logging railroad. (See Thomas T. Tabor in *Tanbark, Alcohol, and Lumber.*)

At 2.5 km (1.6 miles) a spur trail leads to a winter view down Big Mill Creek. This is a view for skiers and is not included in this hike. When the trees are in leaf, you wouldn't see a thing. A clearing will have to be cut to make this view visible year-round.

Continue up the gentle grade to the broad ridgetop. Here you will find sugar maples and black cherry. Black cherry is now even more expensive than walnut for furniture. It isn't appreciated much within the state, but as soon as you cross the border furniture salesmen whisper, "I can get it for you in Pennsylvania in black cherry—for only $1,700 more."

The trail continues to follow an old grade along the top of the ridge, skirting the edge of a clear cut. Next descend to Ellithorpe Run and cross on a bridge. Then turn downstream on a logging railroad grade. This was the longest spur of the railroad on Big Mill Creek and Ellithorpe valley was the last to be cut. By 1925 all the cutting in Elk County was over.

Pass through a small stand of red pine and then turn right to another grade. At 6.0 km (3.7 miles), just after crossing a stream in a culvert, turn right on the Brushy Gap Loop, and climb to a gas well at the top of the hill. Oil production has ceased in the Big Mill Creek Valley, but natural gas production

Bloodroot

continues. Use care to pick up the trail again on the far side of the clearing; then descend gently to a junction with the Challenger Loop. Turn right and then left, crossing the run and passing an old oil well site. Bear left on a grade that slabs the north side of the ridge between Brush Hollow and PA 948. Finally, the trail emerges on the ridgetop.

Pass a grove of plastic tubes. These tubes are used to protect seedlings from being eaten by deer. The interior of the tube retains a lot of moisture, and seedlings are said to grow twice as fast as they would in the open. By the time the tree emerges from the top of the tube, it should be too tough to be eaten. The tubes will then be destroyed by solar ultraviolet radiation. Sugar maples appear to be planted in these tubes.

As you approach the end of the ridge there is a leaves-off view up Big Mill Creek. The trail then switchbacks to the left. This is the most difficult part of the trail system for cross-country skiers. Then pass a year-round view up Big Mill Creek. Next, switch-back to the right, and reach the major trail junction at the end of Brush Hollow. Turn right on the railroad grade, and retrace your steps to the parking lot.

Many additional hiking opportunities are found in this corner of Allegheny National Forest. First is the western part of the Mill Creek Loop Trail. The eastern part of the trail has been closed, so it can no longer be done as a circuit hike. Most of the trees along the eastern part died, letting full sunlight reach the forest floor. Seedlings, brush, and briers sprang up, and keeping the trail open would be a major undertaking. The western part of the loop is still open—you passed the southern end of it on this hike—and it can be hiked either on an in-and-out basis or as a car shuttle from Twin Lakes Recreation Area.

The Buzzard Swamp Trail System (Hike

23) near Marienville provides over 15 kilometers (9 miles) of hiking and cross-country ski trails. Trailheads are on Forest Roads Nos. 157 and 130. There are four or more intersecting loops. Buzzard Swamp provides some of the best wildlife viewing in Allegheny National Forest. With binoculars you may see bear, deer, beaver, coyote, snapping turtles, turkey, osprey, and bald eagles. In the spring migration you might see over 20 species of waterfowl.

The Twin Lakes Trail is a destination trail running 24 kilometers (15 miles) from Twin Lakes Recreation Area to the North Country National Scenic Trail in the Tionesta Scenic Area.

Highway T-397 west of Ridgway provides two additional opportunities for hiking. The 18 kilometers (11 miles) of the Laurel Mill cross-country skiing and hiking area are 5 kilometers (3 miles) west, and the 5 kilometers (3 miles) of the Little Drummer Historical Interpretive Trail are 13 kilometers (8 miles) west. One part of the Little Drummer Trail follows the grade of the Tionesta Valley Railroad.

29

Chapman State Park

Distance: 12.0 km (7.5 miles)

Time: 4 hours

Rise: 287 meters (940 feet)

Highlights: Views; spring wildflowers

Maps: USGS 7½' Cherry Grove, Warren; state park map

Chapman State Park is a pleasant little park of only 324 hectares (800 acres) on the West Branch of Tionesta Creek near Warren. It is bordered by Allegheny National Forest, State Game Land No. 29, and a couple of tracts of private land. The park's trails are unusually well developed but have to be continuously relocated and rebuilt as required by timber sales and oil drilling. The state does not own the oil, gas, or mineral rights under Chapman State Park, and a multitude of oil wells have been drilled in the northern part of the park. Even the federal government owns only 1 to 2 percent of these rights in the giant Allegheny National Forest.

Chapman State Park is at the end of a paved road leading west out of Clarendon on US 6 between Warren and Sheffield. From the turn at the traffic light in Clarendon, it is 5.1 miles to the parking area just below the dam where this hike begins.

Cross the park road to the Penny Run Trail, and squeeze around the gate. The trail is marked with blue paint blazes. This trail was rebuilt by the Youth Conservation Corps in 1980 and mostly uses old roads. It climbs first through hemlocks and open woods. On reaching the border of Allegheny National Forest, it turns right and follows another old road across five bridges to 1.4 km (0.9 mile) where it turns right again and descends along another old road. (Within the national forest the trail is marked with blue-plastic diamonds nailed to the trees.) At 1.7 km (1.1 miles) the trail crosses a bridge over Penny Run. Bear right at 2.2 km (1.4 miles) to reach the paved park road.

Turn left along the park road and follow it to 2.7 km (1.7 miles) where you pass a vehicle

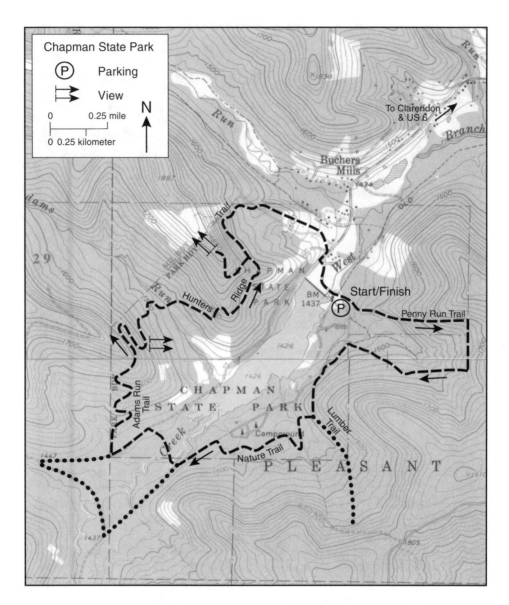

gate and head up the Lumber Trail. In winter the Lumber Trail is used by snowmobiles, hence the sign about Dunham Siding. Keep right where a road goes uphill to the water tank, but turn right at 3.0 km (1.9 miles) on the Nature Trail, which is marked with white paint blazes. Follow the Nature Trail downhill through a hemlock grove. At the bottom cross a stream, and then turn upstream to circle the upper campground loop.

At 3.8 km (2.4 miles) you reach a junction of nature trails. Turn left here and cross a bridge. Turn left again on the Game Lands Trail at 4.3 km (2.7 miles). This trail is the bed of the old Tionesta Valley Railroad. Turn right at 4.5 km (2.9 miles) on the Lowlands Trail, and cross the swinging bridge over the West Branch of Tionesta Creek. At 4.9 km (3.0

The entrance to the Penny Run Trail

miles) turn left on the Adams Run Trail, and follow it almost to the boundary of State Game Land No. 29. There are some green T-shaped blazes along this road.

Then turn right, and switchback up the hill. This part of the Adams Run Trail is mostly marked by yellow paint blazes, but there are some blue ones, as well. The white paint blazes are the boundary of the game lands. It's all very colorful. At the top of the hill this trail picks up a logging road. Follow this to a junction at 6.6 km (4.1 miles). Just before this junction there's a view from a picnic table to the left of the trail. Turn left at the junction, passing a bench. By standing on this bench you can get another glimpse of the lake, but the trees have grown, and the view from the picnic table is better. These are the "over-looks" referred to on the park map.

The Adams Run Trail next passes the first of many oil wells and switchbacks down the hillside to a junction with the Hunters Ridge Trail at 7.5 km (4.7 miles). Follow the blazes very carefully as the hillsides are laced with oil well access roads.

Turn left on the orange-blazed Hunters Ridge Trail, and cross a bridge over Adam's Run. Climb along this trail, which has been rerouted and extended to accommodate the many oil wells, watching very carefully for the blazes. On the far side of the hill turn sharply left at a junction of old roads. Another lake overlook with two picnic tables can be reached by following signs to the left along some of the oil well access roads to the top of the hill. When you're ready to continue the hike, retrace your steps to the Hunters Ridge Trail and turn left on it. The trail now takes you out to the boundary of Game Land No. 29 before descending the hill. Cross Forest Road 437, and continue through an evergreen plantation to the park office. Then follow the roads past the old park office and below the dam to the parking lot where you left your car.

This hike uses almost all the trails in Chapman State Park.

30

Clarion–Little Toby Trail

Distance: 12.6 km (7.5 miles)

Time: 3¾ hours

Rise: 35 meters (120 feet)

Highlights: Ghost towns; mountain streams

Maps: USGS 7½'

The Clarion–Little Toby Trail is a rail trail from Ridgway in Elk County to Brockway in Jefferson County. It follows the bed of the Ridgway-Clearfield branch of the Pennsylvania Railroad that was abandoned in 1968. The northern part of the trail follows the Clarion River next to PA 949 and the CS&X Railroad. This hike is on the southern portion, which follows Little Toby Creek through State Game Lands Nos. 44 and 54. From the old Civilian Conservation Corps (CCC) camp to the ghost town of Carrier, it's devoid of roads and buildings. Like St. Anthony's Wilderness near Harrisburg it was once the site of industrial activity but has now returned to the wild.

The Clarion–Little Toby Trail requires a lengthy but straightforward car shuttle—29.2 miles—which suggests that the trail could also be hiked on an in-and-out basis from either end. The trail can be reached from exit 97 on I-80. Drive north on US 219 for 7.6 miles to Brockway. Turn left on PA 28 (Main Street) at the traffic light for 0.4 miles, and then turn right on 7th Avenue where there's a sign for Toby Terrace. Drive north for 2.8 miles, passing the southern end of the trail, to a parking lot at Jenkins Run. Leave one car, and return to Brockway and the junction of PA 28 and US 219. Follow US 219 north for 17.5 miles to Ridgway. In downtown Ridgway turn south on PA 949—Ignore PA 948—and follow it for 7.7 miles to the signed turnoff on the left. Follow this road south for 0.8 mile, and park just beyond the old CCC camp.

To start your hike, head south on the old railroad grade, crossing Laurel Run. Lots of

Rusted remains at the Garocii Quarry

skunk cabbage grows in the lowlands along Laurel Run. The active CS&X Railroad is safely on the far side of Little Toby Creek. Trees found along the valley are yellow birch, black cherry, black birch, beech, hemlock, red and white oak, and red maple. Red maple, also called swamp maple, used to be found only in swamps. It is very sensitive to fire damage, and now that forest fires are suppressed, it's expanding its range. Indeed, this swamp thing is now found everywhere in Penn's Woods, which are becoming a red-maple monoculture.

At 1.0 km (0.6 mile) there are two fenced areas to the right of the trail. They may be deer exclosures. Pennsylvania's deer population is so high that many plants and the birds and animals dependent on them are severely reduced in numbers. A deer exclosure area shows what the vegetation would be like without all the Bambis browsing on it.

The ruins of the Garocii stone crusher are reached at 2.0 km (1.2 miles). A yellow-blazed side trail about 1.0 km (0.6 mile) long leads to the quarry. Next you pass the site of the ghost town of Grove and its train station. At least six ghost towns are found in this valley. In all, there are estimated to be over 1,000 ghost towns in the commonwealth. When populated, most of these towns were small and associated with various extractive industries. But Pithole City, to the west of here, reached a population of 10,000 in 1865, just before the oil wells started to go dry. Unlike in the arid southwest, wood doesn't last in Pennsylvania, and if the town hadn't established its own graveyard, the only thing left might be the town dump and perhaps some cellar holes. Every town had a dump.

Cross Coward Run at 2.7 km (1.7 miles) and reach Shorts Mill, another ghost town, just beyond. Then pass the site of a Dec-

Allegheny National Forest

ember 1932 train wreck. Just two coal cars—it wouldn't have even made CNN. At 3.6 km (2.2 miles) there are some rhododendrons at the top of the bank. The silence of the valley is broken only by the sounds of Little Toby Creek.

At 6.1 km (3.8 miles) there's a scattered grove of white pines and a swinging bridge over the creek between the stone abutments of a much larger 19th-century bridge. The swinging bridge follows the catenary curve of the supporting cables. The tension in these cables has to be increased to reduce the sag of the bridge. The ghost town of Blue Rock was located nearby.

Cross Vineyard Run at 7.9 km (4.9 miles). The ghost town here was associated with a sawmill. Next pass a grove of larch trees and cross Little Vineyard Run. At 8.9 km (5.5 miles) there are cliffs to the left, and the railroad grade enters a cut. Note the wild apple tree growing on the bank opposite milepost 14. Did some trainman toss out his apple core here and thus plant a tree?

At 9.5 km (5.9 miles) leave the state game land and pass the first of many hunting camps. Then pass the ghost town of Carrier. Note the stone bridge abutments and pier to the right.

At 11.0 km (6.8 miles) the old railroad grade was incorporated into a landowner's yard. The trail bypasses on a new alignment. Turn left to the parking lot just before Jenkins Run.

This hike could be extended 3.5 km (2.2 miles) to the southern trailhead at Taylor Park in Brockway but only 1.1 km (0.7 mile) to Carman Siding at the north end.

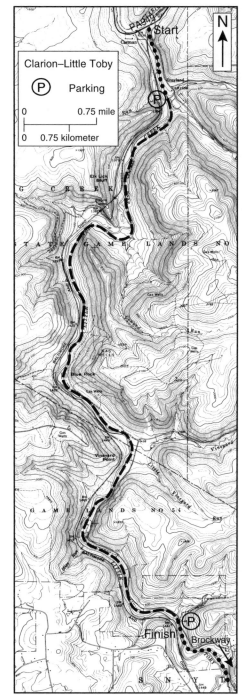

31

Tracy Ridge Trail

Distance: 16.7 km (10.3 miles)

Time: 5½ hours

Rise: 360 meters (1,200 feet)

Highlight: North Country Trail

Maps: USGS 7½' Cornplanter Run, Stickney; Allegheny National Forest Hiking Guide, *map 1*

Another large roadless area in Allegheny National Forest is Tracy Ridge in the northern part of the forest, just south of the New York border. The area is bounded by PA 321 on the east, Willow Bay Recreational Area on the north, Allegheny Reservoir on the west, and Sugar Bay on the south. Tracy Ridge has been granted National Recreation Area status.

This hike is a daylong circuit, following parts of the Johnnycake and North Country Trails as well as Tracy Ridge. The hike could be turned into a two-day backpack by using the Handsome Lake campground, south of Johnnycake Run on the North Country Trail. Due to the length of the trail, hiking boots are recommended.

The Tracy Ridge Trail parking lot is on the west side of PA 321, 2.6 miles south of the junction with PA 346, 0.4 mile north of the entrance to Tracy Ridge campground, and 11.0 miles north of the junction with PA 59.

Start your hike by stepping over the log restricting motor access to an old fire road and begin on the Tracy Ridge Trail. In addition to the motorized vehicles whose decals are shown on the trailhead bulletin board, mountain bikes are also prohibited on this trail. At 0.3 km (0.2 mile) turn left on a trail that's marked with white-plastic diamonds. The blue "eye" blazes, once popular in Allegheny National Forest, are still in evidence, and you will need them both to follow this trail. The "eye" blazes consist of a small horizontal rectangle above a larger vertical rectangle. When done correctly on reasonably smooth bark, they resemble the letter "i." They do avoid confusion with trees marked for sale but create problems at turns and intersections.

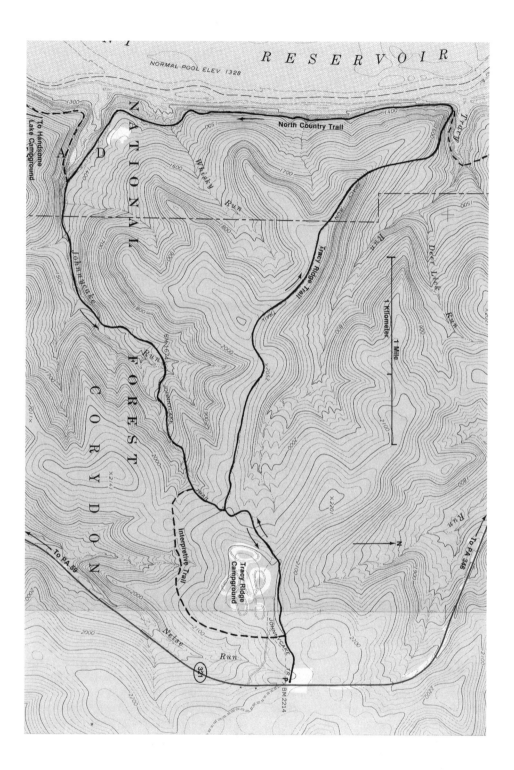

The Appalachian Trail itself was originally marked with 5-centimeter copper diamonds with the letters AT pricked out. The copper diamonds didn't last long and were soon replaced with the familiar white paint blazes. It is a sad fact of life, but trail marking must be vandal-resistant. In Allegheny National Forest this historic progression has been reversed, and trail marking has become more vulnerable to vandalism.

At 0.8 km (0.5 mile) bear right where the Interpretive Trail comes in from the left. The Interpretive Trail is also marked with white diamonds, but some of them have become tattletale gray. There are some old green "eye" blazes, as well. Partway past some big rocks at 1.2 km (0.8 mile) the trail turns sharp left and proceeds through a narrow passage. The campground is visible through the trees. Beyond the rocks, you bear right. You reach the Johnnycake Trail junction at 2.2 km (1.4 miles). This is the trail that you'll return on. Note the casing of an old oil well in this clearing. Turn right and continue on Tracy Ridge Trail. Tracy Ridge is broad and flat, so you don't begin to see its edge until you are well along. As the ridge narrows, you swing over the left side to start down to Allegheny Reservoir. This is a new trail, built to avoid a steep drop down the ridgeline itself. Soon you swing back to the ridgeline and continue to descend. The trail becomes rough and obscure, so follow the blazes carefully.

At 6.7 km (4.2 miles)—the bottom of the hill—you reach a junction with the North Country Trail now marked with blue diamonds. To your right, the North Country Trail leads to Allegany State Park in New York (yes, there is a different spelling on the other side of the state line). The North Country Trail climbs across the steep hillside that drops into the reservoir that can be seen through the trees.

Along the hillside you cross a number of streams of various sizes. Whisky Run is the largest of these, and you cross it at 9.4 km (5.8 miles) but it appears to have been misnamed. At 10.1 km (6.3 miles) you pass through an open grove of white pines. The North Country Trail now swings eastward in order to round Johnnycake Run inlet on the reservoir. Johnnycake Trail and Run are reached at 10.6 km (6.6 miles). The North Country Trail crosses the run and continues to Handsome Lake campground—and eventually to North Dakota. A vista over the reservoir has been cut just south of Johnnycake Bay. Turn left and follow the blue-blazed Johnnycake Trail upstream along an old road under hemlocks. Johnnycake Trail is marked with white-plastic diamonds and old blue "eye" blazes.

At 11.4 km (7.1 miles) note evidence of an old corduroy road at a side stream crossing. Johnnycake Run itself is crossed at 11.7 km (7.3 miles) and again at 12.1 km (7.6 miles). A bit farther up the hill beware of a trail to the left marked with white diamonds but not with blue "eye" blazes. This new trail has no footway. At 14.2 km (8.9 miles) you pass a junction with the Interpretive Trail on your right, and at the top of the hill you bear right on the Tracy Ridge Trail. From here you retrace your steps to your car.

This hike could be extended by following the North Country Trail either to the north or south. The only other hike appears to be the 4-km (2.5-mile) Interpretive Trail around the campground.

The Morrison Trail on PA 59 resembles this hike in many respects. The Morrison Trail was built by the Allegheny Outdoor Club, but without consulting the club the Allegheny National Forest opened it to mountain bikes. Because of the resulting risk to hikers on this narrow, steep trail, the Morrison Trail is no longer included in this book.

32

Hickory Creek Trail

Distance: 18.7 km (11.6 miles)

Time: 7 hours

Rise: 315 meters (1,030 feet)

Highlights: Pennsylvania's only congressionally designated wilderness area; old logging camp

Maps: USGS 7½' Cobham; U.S. Forest Service map

Hickory Creek Trail is located within a large roadless area in Allegheny National Forest and contained in the wedge of land between East Hickory and Middle Hickory Creeks. Hickory Creek has been accorded wilderness status by Congress; therefore, please keep group sizes small—and note that no mountain bikes or motorized vehicles are permitted. If you find historic artifacts in the wilderness, leave them along the trail for others to enjoy.

Although roadless today, the area was not always so. Nearly every valley contains the bed of a logging railroad, while old skid roads and more recent jeep trails lace the hillsides. The area was logged by Wheeler and Dusenbury of Endeavor, starting around 1910. Beginning in 1837, this company lumbered in Pennsylvania and New York for over a century.

Instead of doing Hickory Creek as a long day hike, many people prefer to turn it into a backpack of two or more days. With just a daypack you can probably shave an hour or more off the hiking time, but backpackers will need the full seven hours on the trail. If you backpack, please camp at least 50 meters from the trail and from any stream. Practice minimal impact techniques. Due to the length of the trail hiking boots are recommended.

The trailhead is at Hearts Content Picnic Area. Hearts Content is most easily reached from SR 3005 at a junction 10.3 miles from PA 62 at Tidioute and 10.9 miles from US 6 at Warren. Turn south on Hearts Content–Sheffield Road (SR 2002). Another 3.7 miles brings you to the trailhead. Drinking water is available at the picnic area during the summer. Yellow paint "eye" blazes—so named because

A meadow along the Hickory Creek Trail

they resemble the letter "i"—are used to mark the Hickory Creek Trail. Rejoice that they have not been replaced with plastic markers.

When you start, the trail quickly traverses a red pine plantation and then crosses Hearts Content Road. On the far side of the road it passes under the junction of two pole lines and joins the loop at 1.0 km (0.6 mile) from the start. Continue ahead for the south side through characteristically open woods. The very openness of the woods forces you to keep a sharp lookout for the paint blazes because the footway may fade out. But the footing is fairly even and the walking easy as you swing along, generally downhill.

You cross a woods road at 1.3 km (0.8 mile) and pass a spring to the right at 1.7 km (1.1 miles). At 2.4 km (1.5 miles) you cross a nameless tributary of Middle Hickory Creek as best you can, and immediately beyond you cross an old logging road.

Begin a gradual climb at 3.1 km (1.9 miles). The trail continues gently up and down as it follows the edge of the plateau. Trees along this stretch are black cherry, beech, maple, red oak, and hemlock.

Just beyond 5.6 km (3.5 miles) you cross an old road and a dry watercourse, and then you bear left on another old road for a stretch. A large meadow along Coon Run is reached at 6.2 km (3.8 miles). You then cross a Coon tributary and head downstream along the edge of the meadow.

The meadows along Coon Run offer opportunities for camping, and you'll see several campsites along the trail. Cross Coon Run itself at 7.0 km (4.4 miles), and climb gently away from the run.

Continue the gradual climb into the next watershed. At 8.6 km (5.4 miles) cross an open swath. It looks like just another gas pipeline, but according to the USFS map this is an old artillery range. It's said to date from World War I when cannons were tested here and was to have been "cleaned up," but I got the impression that those who actually

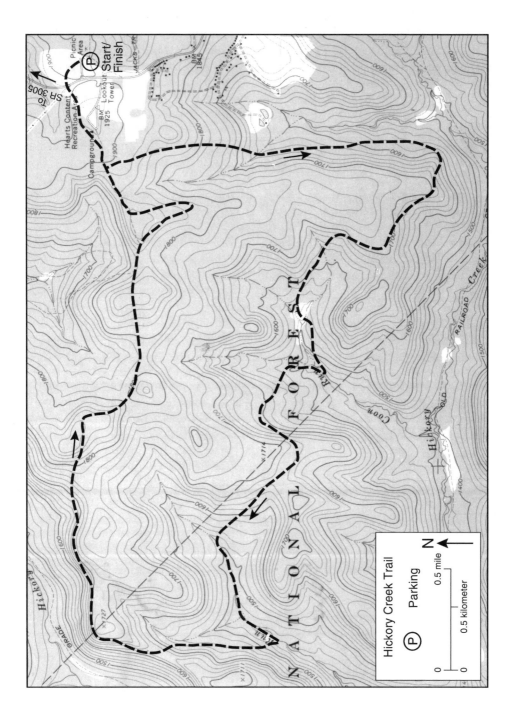

Hickory Creek Trail

Ⓟ Parking

N

0   0.5 kilometer

0   0.5 mile

know something about this range don't want to talk about it. Stick to the trail and step softly across this area. *Don't pick up anything* but if you see something that looks like an artillery shell, mark the spot and report it to the Bradford ranger office.

Next, jog left across an old road, and then cross a few streams at 9.3 km (5.8 miles) and continue past a meadow to your right. Among other trees growing here is yellow birch.

Soon you are following an old logging railroad grade along Jacks Run. Note the parallel depressions across the grade where the uncreosoted ties rotted in place. These depressions are one of the surest signs of an old railroad grade, which can be hard to identify since most of them were never mapped. This one appears to have been standard gauge. In one cut the old ties can still be seen. There are more opportunities for camping along this stream.

The ruins of an old logging camp can be found along Jacks Run. The camp was of unusual design in that it was all under one roof, like a railroad flat. Ironwork from school desks was found here. Was there once a small school in the midst of this now roadless area?

There are only a couple of stream crossings as the trail follows Jacks Run for about 1 km. At the last crossing, turn right and start the gentle climb to the broad ridge between East and Middle Hickory Creeks.

At a saddle in the ridge the trail switches to the far side and continues to climb, reaching the top of the hill at 11.9 km (7.4 miles). There are some leaves-off views over the valley of East Hickory Creek from this section. At 12.5 km (7.8 miles) cross a small stream, and at 13.3 km (8.3 miles) swing away from the edge of the ridge, cross another small stream, and start to climb again. Now swing right, along the base of a slope, and continue on among large boulders.

At 14.0 km (8.8 miles) you are back to an edge that drops off to the left. Cross another old railroad grade at 16.0 km (10.0 miles). These landmarks are followed by a woods road at 16.6 km (10.4 miles), and at 17.7 km (11.1 miles) you've returned to the loop junction. Turn left, and it's 1.0 km (0.6 mile) back to the trailhead and your car.

To actually see Hickory Creek itself, you would have to follow one of the routes in the Sierra Club book *Allegheny National Forest Hiking Guide.* However, these routes are not marked or maintained.

Other hikes in the Hickory Creek vicinity can be found on the nearby Tanbark Trail, Hearts Content Scenic Area, and some shorter trails.

Pittsburgh and the Southwest

Slippery Rock Gorge Trail

33

Wolf Creek Narrows Natural Area

Distance: 2.4 km (1.5 mile)

Time: ¾ hour

Rise: 43 meters (140 feet)

Highlight: Spring wildflowers

Maps: USGS 7½' Slippery Rock; Western Pennsylvania Conservancy brochure map

Wolf Creek Narrows, near Slippery Rock in Butler County, is one of the more recent acquisitions of the Western Pennsylvania Conservancy. When I first visited the area, I had to cross a piece of private land between the road and the Conservancy tract that was open to conservancy members only. Three months later the conservancy purchased that private land, so the trail to Wolf Creek Narrows Natural Area is now open to the public.

The big attraction of Wolf Creek Narrows is its wildflowers in late April and early May. It can be a very pretty trail at any time of year, but in spring not only is the ground carpeted with wildflowers, but you also get the best views of the creek before the trees leaf out. Laying out trails in a new natural area is painful since you can't avoid destroying some of the wildflowers you are trying to save. But it has to be done. Without established trails, "herd paths" might well destroy even more.

The trailhead for Wolf Creek Narrows is 1.7 miles west of PA 258 in Slippery Rock, on West Water Street. Cross the bridge over Wolf Creek, and take the first left. Parking is permitted just inside the fringe of trees along the road, but please don't block the lane, and don't park along the paved road. Ordinary walking shoes should be fine for this short hike.

To start, walk back across the bridge, and turn left on the signed trail at the end of the bridge abutment. The white-blazed trail takes you upstream along Wolf Creek into the bulk of the Natural Area. Keep a

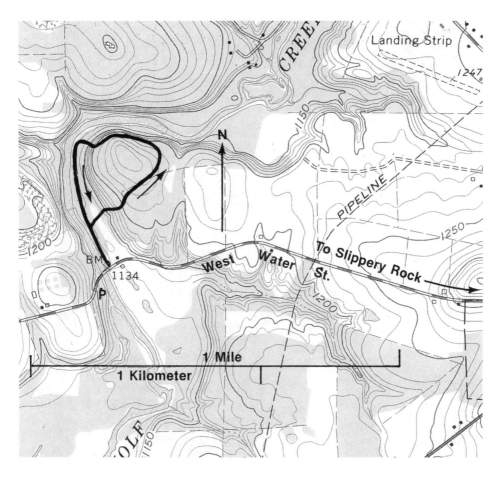

sharp eye out for the loop-trail junction, where you turn right and follow the trail across the bottomland to the base of the hill. Many of the best wildflowers are found on the south slope of the hill. Trees growing on this slope are black cherry, hemlock, beech, maple, basswood, and black gum. In late April abundant wild-flowers are hepatica, mayapple, and trillium. Follow the blazes carefully on top of the hill because half of them have been blacked out, possibly in the belief that the trail was overblazed.

At 1.0 km (0.6 mile) turn left above the narrows. Glimpses of Wolf Creek can be seen between the trees. Soon you reach the edge of the hill and descend to the creek, which runs on bedrock at this point. The trail continues along the edge of the stream and under the hemlocks, with views of the small cliffs in the limestone on the far side. At 1.9 km (1.2 miles) you close the loop trail and retrace your steps to your car.

The conservancy tract includes an area on the far side of Wolf Creek. It has no marked trails and can be reached only by fording the creek. The Jennings Nature Reserve, on the other side of Slippery Rock at the junction of PA 8 and PA 173, offers additional trails and wildflowers (see Hike 34).

34

Jennings Environmental Education Center

Distance: 3.5 km (2.2 miles)

Time: 1¾ hours

Rise: 75 meters (240 feet)

Highlights: Prairie wildflowers; massasauga rattlesnakes

Maps: USGS 7½' Slippery Rock; park map

Although most of Pennsylvania was heavily wooded at the time of settlement, there were a few bits of prairie, remnants from a period of higher temperatures about 4,000 years ago when the tall grass prairies expanded to the east. Here, on the beach of glacial Lake Edmund, was one of them. Found here are plants of western prairies, particularly the blazing star, which blooms in late July and early August and is worth a special trip. Many other wildflowers, including woodland varieties, also occur at Jennings. So a visit anytime from early spring to fall will likely find something in bloom. In all, 386 species of plants have been observed at Jennings. The more people look, the more they find.

The occurrence of the blazing star on a tract of only 3 acres was recognized by Dr. Otto E. Jennings, a botanist and educator. Dr. Jennings succeeded in getting the Western Pennsylvania Conservancy to purchase this 125-hectare (310-acre) tract containing the tiny relict prairie. By clearing portions of the adjacent woodland, the prairie has since been expanded to about 12 hectares (30 acres). The bulk of the area remains wooded. Subsequently, the Western Pennsylvania Conservancy transferred the area to public ownership, and it is now operated by the Bureau of State Parks as an environmental education center.

The center is also home to the massasauga rattlesnake. The massasauga is shorter than the timber rattlesnake, prefers to live in swamps, and is shy and retiring. Stay on the established trails so you won't

New York ironweed

meet the massasauga unexpectedly. Should you be lucky enough to spot this elusive reptile, observe it from a distance with binoculars or a telephoto lens. The massasauga is endangered in Pennsylvania and consequently protected.

Jennings is located at the junction of PA 8, PA 173 and PA 528, about 12.0 miles north of Butler, 4.0 miles south of Slippery Rock, and adjacent to the boundary of Moraine State Park. You can park in either of the lots at Jennings, but the one on the north side of PA 528 adjacent to the prairie is more convenient for this hike. The trails at Jennings have been hardened in recent years to reduce the amount of mud, so good walking shoes are fine for this hike.

To start, walk between the pillars marking the entrance to the Blazing Star Self-Guided Nature Trail. Note the flowing, or artesian, well to the right of these pillars. After only 65 meters (70 yards) of this graveled path you enter the prairie at the junction of the Massasauga Trail, on which you will return at the end of your hike. Look here for the blazing star. Note the evidence of man-made fire required to keep the forest from returning. Shortly, you pass the Prairie Loop Trail on your right, which you could take to lengthen your stay among the prairie wildflowers. The loop would add only 0.4 km (0.3 mile) to your hike. At the far side of the prairie bear right on the Deer Trail. Trail junctions are all signed at Jennings. Next at 0.6 km (0.4 mile) bear right on the Oakwoods Trail.

You will pass several old pits to the left of the trail. Just what was sought here remains a mystery, and recent excavation failed to find anything of value. Speculation now centers on clay for a long-gone pottery. To the right of the trail, three rows of daffodils give seasonal evidence of a vanished homestead.

At 1.4 km (0.9 mile) the trail follows the boundary of private land. Shagbark hickory,

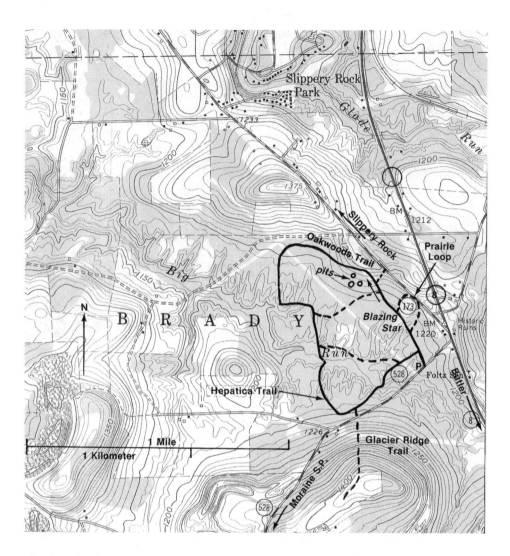

shingle oak, white oak, and black cherry are frequent trees along this section. Next, the trail follows along a small stream before crossing it on bridge.

Just after rounding a corner of private land, the old field trail diverges to the left. Continue along the fence, descend into the bottoms bordering Big Run, and cross a bridge over a wet area. At 2.4 km (1.5 miles) turn right on Hepatica Trail, and cross Big Run on another bridge.

Beyond Big Run the Hepatica Trail climbs up the stream bank. It then reaches a junction with the former route of the Glacier Ridge Trail, now white-blazed.

Turn left on the old Glacier Ridge Trail. After recrossing Big Run, look for gabians (wire baskets filled with rocks) used to stabilize the stream bank. At 3.2 km (2.0 miles) turn right on the Massasauga Trail, which passes a picnic pavilion and continues along the edge of the prairie to a junction with the Blazing Star Trail. Turn right here, and it's just a few steps to the parking lot.

There are further opportunities for walking at Jennings. This hike has bypassed a number of trails that could be used to truncate or extend it. To the south of PA 528, a circuit hike can be made on the Old Mill, Black Cherry, and Ridge Trails. Just across PA 8 is the Old Stone House, a replica of a stagecoach inn dating from the 1820s. Guests—who ranged from counterfeiters to the Marquis de Lafayette—were required to remove their boots in bed but were promised that there would be no more than five people per bed.

35

Wildflower Reserve

Distance: 3.9 km (2.4 miles)

Time: 1½ hours

Rise: 30 meters (100 feet)

Highlight: Wildflowers

Maps: USGS 7½' Aliquippa, Clinton; state park map

Raccoon Creek State Park is located in Beaver County, about 25 miles west of Pittsburgh. It is a large park by Pennsylvania standards and was established by the National Park Service back in the Great Depression through the acquisition of submarginal farmland. Ruins of some of these farms can still be found in the undeveloped western portions of the park. Despite its name, most of the park occupies the valley of Traverse Creek. This hike is in the only part of the park on Raccoon Creek, in the small portion east of US 30 set aside as a wildflower reserve. Originally purchased by the Western Pennsylvania Conservancy, it was transferred to the state in 1971.

The only entrance to the wildflower reserve is from US 30, about 3.0 miles west of Clinton. Pets are not permitted on the trails of the wildflower reserve, so do your pet a favor and don't bring it. Then you won't have to leave it in your car while you hike. Drive through the evergreen plantation and park. If time permits—and this is a short, easy hike—stop in at the nature center. The trails might be a little muddy, but ordinary walking shoes should be fine. The best time to visit Raccoon Creek for spring wildflowers is the second week of May. Note that additional trails are being established in the Wildflower Reserve.

The hike starts on the Jennings Trail at the far end of the parking area. (The Jennings Trail has the greatest variety of plant life, and it also intersects many other trails, permitting you to vary or truncate this hike.) Moving along the Jennings Trail, you climb a small hill and then circle around

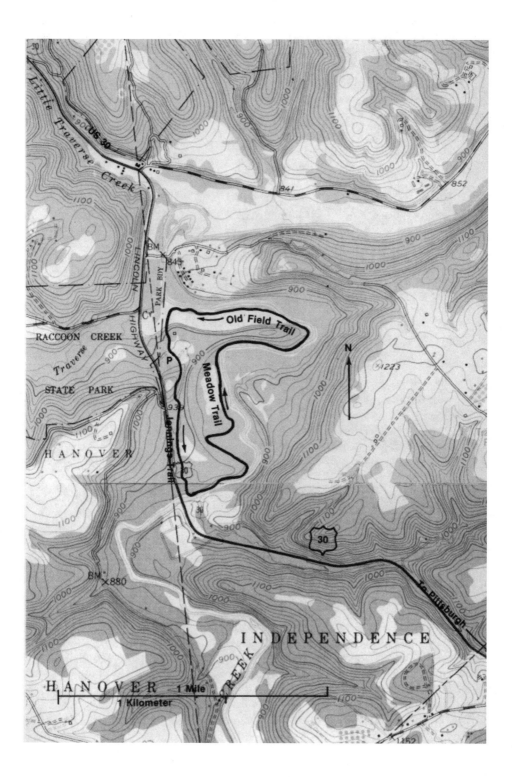

Jack-in-the-pulpit

Hungerford Cabin. Hungerford was a cartoonist for the *Pittsburgh Press and Post Gazette,* and this cabin was his second home. Second homes were modest in those days. Beyond the clearing, use the switchbacks to descend the slope. At 0.4 km (0.2 mile) the Deer Trail goes left, and shortly the Big Maple Trail does the same. Along this section you can see woodland wildflowers such as mayapples and hepatica. These wildflowers must grow and bloom in the few short weeks of spring before the deciduous trees leaf out and block the sunlight. At 0.6 km (0.4 mile) the trail crosses a small stream, and at 0.8 km (0.5 mile) it reaches the top of a low cliff. Bear right and descend the steps. Ridge Trail continues ahead at this point. You may notice some poison ivy along the trail.

In these bottomlands look for trillium and Virginia bluebell. Also note the wood duck box on a post in the slough. A great many bird boxes have been installed in the wildflower reserve, and they are all worth a hard look, since they might have interesting tenants. Different species of trees grow here in the bottomland. Largest of these is the sycamore, with its peeling light-colored bark. The silence on the bottomland is frequently broken by jets from the Greater Pittsburgh Airport.

The Jennings Trail hugs the base of the upland. At 1.4 km (0.9 mile) you turn full right on the Old Wagon Road Trail, which takes you out onto the bottomland toward Raccoon Creek. At 1.6 km (1.0 mile) you bear left on the Meadow Trail and, appropriately, enter a large meadow on the bottomland. The open meadow is a very different environment. Here one may find wildflowers blooming in the summer and fall. Bird boxes might harbor the rare eastern bluebird. Ignore the Hickory Trail.

At 2.1 km (1.3 miles) turn right on the Jennings Trail again at an unsigned junction, which lies between the base of the cliffs and Raccoon Creek. Note the large tulip trees growing on the bottomland. Here the Beaver Trail makes an optional loop to the right—but beaver cuttings are not guaranteed.

At 2.7 km (1.7 miles) you turn right on the Old Field Trail at the junction with the Audubon Trail. This trail takes you back to the creek and then between the creek and the old field. Here there *are* old beaver cuttings. Ignore a cutoff trail, and then bear right at a trail junction. The Travis Trail makes another optional loop to the right. Circle back to a junction with the Henrici Trail at 3.7 km (2.3 miles). Henrici was an outdoor writer from Sewickly. Turn right and climb the steps up the hill. At the top, bear right on the road. The parking lot is visible ahead.

There are additional hiking opportunities in the western portion of Raccoon Creek State park on the Wetland, Valley, and Frankfort Mineral Springs Trails.

36

Beechwood Nature Trails

Distance: 4.0 km (2.5 miles)

Time: 1¾ hours

Rise: 115 meters (380 feet)

Highlight: A pleasant walk

Maps: USGS 7½' Glenshaw; Nature Reserve map (available at Evans Nature Center)

Beechwood Farms is a small nature reserve within the Pittsburgh metropolitan area, owned by the Western Pennsylvania Conservancy and operated by the Western Pennsylvania Audubon Society. Because of its many steep-walled valleys, Pittsburgh has an abundance of undeveloped land that frequently serves as a refuge for wildlife. Beechwood, a tract of upland once operated as a dairy farm, is being permitted to return to its natural state.

Beechwood Farms can be reached from exit 39 on the Pennsylvania Turnpike. Go south on PA 8 for 3.0 miles, and then turn left on the Green Belt, which at this point is Harts Run Road. The Green Belt is one of several systems of roads that encircle Pittsburgh. Follow the Green Belt for 3.7 miles, and then turn right on the Dorseyville Road at a stop sign and T-junction. Another 0.3 mile brings you to the Beechwood parking lot, just across from the Fox Chapel fire department.

Walking shoes are fine for this short hike. Don't forget your binoculars for a little birding. Poison ivy no longer presents the hazard at Beechwood that it did some years ago.

Dogs are prohibited on the trails at Beechwood; leave Rover at home so you won't have to lock him in your car. If the Evans Nature Center is open, visitors should register. There are plenty of exhibits, and you can go down the stairs to the basement where the rest rooms are found, and then use the back door to reach the trails.

If the Nature Center is not open, pass between the buildings to reach the trailhead map board.

Mighty oaks

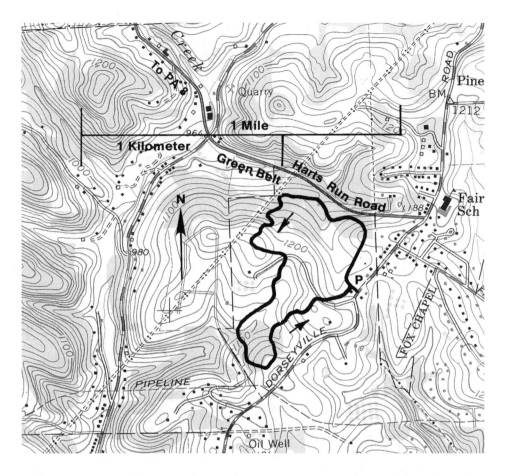

Starting at the trailhead sign, bear right on a mowed path through the meadow, which affords a view of the farm pond. Then turn right at the edge of the woods, and continue ahead on the yellow-blazed Oak Forest Trail. The Oak Forest Trail is crossed and then recrossed by a bridle trail.

Continue through woods that contain dogwood and shadbush as well as various oaks. This trail makes a close approach to Harts Run Road, which you can see through the trees even with the leaves on.

At 0.6 km (0.4 mile) turn right on the yellow-blazed Spring Hollow Walk. (Trail junctions are signed at Beechwood.) Descend next to an old eroded road. Cross Harts Run on a bridge, and then start the climb back to the uplands.

At 0.8 km (0.5 mile) continue ahead on the white-blazed Woodland Trail, which switchbacks up the hill, passing through an evergreen plantation. It comes very close to a power line swath at one point. Turn left at the top of the hill, and descend to a meadow.

Turn right on Meadow View Trail at 1.6 km (1.0 mile) and then cross a private driveway. Turn right again on Pine Hollow Trail at 1.9 km (1.2 miles). You soon enter the woods and cross Beechwood Run on what was an old driveway and is now a red-blazed bridle path.

At 2.4 km (1.5 miles) cross an old dam which has completely silted in. The dam was built at the brink of a waterfall, so the silt isn't as deep as it appears. Then climb through an evergreen plantation. Red pines are encountered first, then white pines, and finally larch trees. On the way down this hill a band of Norway spruce is added.

Cross the bridle trail again where it follows a pole line. Then turn right on Meadow View Trail at 3.5 km (2.2 miles). You pass a number of mulberry trees—always a favorite of fruit-eating birds. Shortly, turn left for Meadow View Lookout, only 40 meters down the side trail, which provides a view across the meadows of Beechwood Farms.

Back on the Meadow View Trail, you cross the private drive, and then turn right on Spring Hollow Walk. Soon you are back at the Evans Nature Center and your car.

37

Harrison Hills Park

In-and-out distance: 4.0 km (2.5 miles)

Time: 1½ hours

Rise: 115 meters (380 feet)

Highlights: Views; Rachel Carson Trail

Maps: USGS 7½' Freeport; Rachel Carson Trail maps (available from Hosteling International, Pittsburgh)

Harrison Hills Park is in the extreme northeast corner of Allegheny County on the bluffs above the Allegheny River. In 1949 members of the newly formed Pittsburgh Council of the American Youth Hostels were on a canoe trip on the Allegheny, and the cliffs inspired them to build a cross-country foot trail from Pittsburgh to Cook Forest State Park. The trail was named after Horace Forbes Baker, who established the Pittsburgh Council shortly before his death. Originally the Baker Trail started at the Highland Park bridge over the Allegheny, but rapid development soon forced abandonment of all 40 kilometers (25 miles) of the trail in Allegheny County.

An attempt was made in the early seventies to salvage parts of the original Baker Trail and weld them into a new trail across northern Allegheny County. This trail passes close to the birthplace of Rachel Carson, the famous environmentalist. Rachel Carson is known best for her books *The Sea Around Us* (1951) and *Silent Spring* (1962). The latter warned of the dangers of herbicides and pesticides, particularly DDT.

A 53-kilometer (33-mile) trail was finally blazed, stretching from North Park to Harrison Hills, mostly on private land. This hike takes you along one of the few sections on public land. It is also part of the original Baker Trail.

Harrison Hills Park is reached from PA 28. From the north take exit 16, and drive east 0.6 mile to Freeport Road. Turn right, go another 0.9 mile, and turn left into the park. From the south take exit 15, and turn right on Burtner Road for 0.8 mile. Turn left

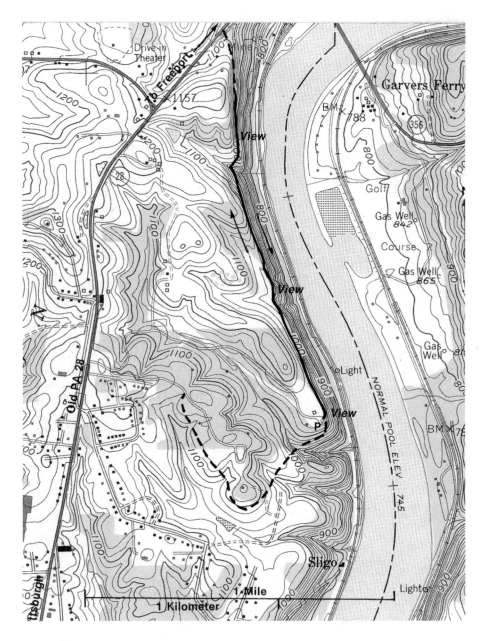

on Freeport Road at the light in Birdville. Turn right into the park 0.5 mile beyond the traffic light for Highlands Mall. Just inside the park entrance take the left fork of the road, and follow it to its end in a parking lot (one of several near the cliffs), about 0.9 mile from the highway. Drinking water and rest rooms are available at the picnic area. There is some poison ivy along the trail, and the cliffs are unforgiving. Keep a tight hold

---

A view of the Allegheny River

on children and dogs. Walking shoes are fine despite some wet places, but you will appreciate the lug soles of hiking boots on some steep slopes.

Begin from the parking lot, heading across the open area past the picnic shelter to a break in the trees that provides a leaves-off view across the Allegheny into Westmoreland County. Then turn left and pick up the yellow blazes of the Rachel Carson Trail where it heads into the woods, passing the Michael Watts Memorial Overlook. Mr. Watts was a native of Pittsburgh who worked to restore clean water to the rivers and streams of western Pennsylvania. The trail pops back into the picnic area again before committing itself to the woods.

Generally the path you want is the one closer to the edge of the cliffs. A heavily used jogging trail diverges to the left after a bit. At 0.7 km (0.4 mile) you cross a stream on a bridge; you can hear the stream cascading over the cliff beyond.

Shortly, another side stream is encountered. At 1.3 km (0.8 mile) there's a view of the PA 356 bridge at Freeport and the new marina across the Allegheny. Basswood trees and serviceberries grow right at the brink. Next, you descend steeply and continue north below the edge of the bluffs. The tree with the blaze you need at this point is lying on the ground about halfway down the slope. Cross a stream in a deep ravine at 1.5 km (0.9 mile) and then climb back to the top of the hill. You reach a walled spring at 1.9 km (1.2 miles). To my surprise I walked up on a turkey who was scratching up a meal right on the Rachel Carson Trail. It took off, keeping a large tree between us. Continue until the trail emerges on a gravel road. From here on it crosses backyards so turn and retrace your steps to your car.

Other hiking opportunities at Harrison Hills can be found by following the Rachel Carson Trail the other way out to Freeport Road.

38

McConnells Mill State Park

Distance: 5.2 km (3.2 miles)

Time: 2 hours

Rise: 103 meters (340 feet)

Highlights: Gorge; waterfalls; rapids; wildflowers; old mill; covered bridge

Maps: USGS 7½' Portersville; state park map

Geologically, the gorge of Slippery Rock Creek is quite recent, dating only from the last ice age. Before the ice age, Slippery Rock and Muddy Creeks both flowed northwest to the St. Lawrence River. But with their way blocked by the continental ice sheet, large lakes formed in the valleys of the creeks. As the ice began to retreat, glacial Lake Arthur found a new outlet here, and the enormous flow of meltwater cut this gorge in only a few thousand years. Today, Slippery Rock Creek flows to the Ohio, and its gorge has become one of the few unspoiled hemlock ravines in the western part of the state. Twelve species of ferns are found at McConnells Mill State Park, more than anywhere else in western Pennsylvania.

McConnells Mill State Park is about 40 miles north of Pittsburgh, just 0.3 mile west of the junction of US 422 with US 19 and 1.7 miles west of Exit 99 on I-79. Turn south off US 422, and it's another 0.7 mile to the parking lot at the Johnson Road junction, where this hike begins. In driving south from US 422, you cross two of the sites where glacial Lake Arthur drained into Slippery Rock Gorge.

Good walking shoes are adequate for this hike. This hike is best avoided in winter, because seep springs coat the rocks with ice, and footing becomes extremely treacherous. The spring wildflowers are usually at their peak around the third week in May.

To start your hike, walk north along the road about 100 meters (330 feet) to the Alpha Pass trailhead. A small stream flows over the edge of the Homewood Sandstone here, creating a small waterfall. This is one

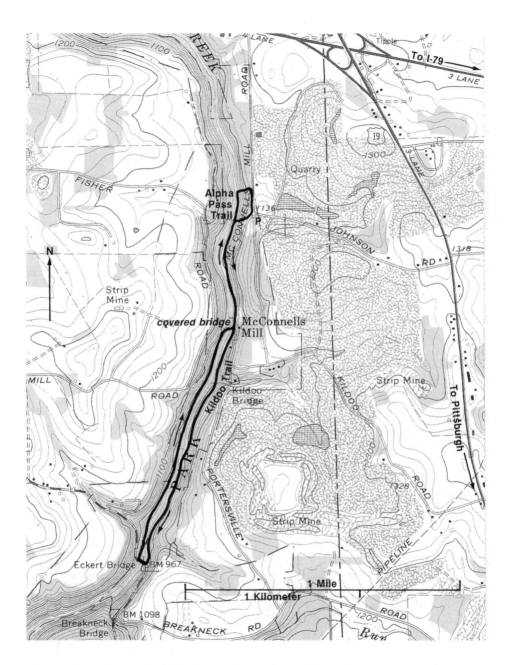

of the sites where glacial Lake Arthur drained its torrent into the gorge. At that time the ground here would have shaken under your feet. Head down the steep but short Alpha Pass Trail, and reach the trail along the creek in another 100 meters. There are several opportunities here to view the rapids in Slippery Rock Creek from the large blocks of sandstone that have slid down the side of the gorge.

Turn left and head downstream on this rough trail. At 0.5 km (0.3 mile) you pass a junction with the trail that you'll use at the end of your hike. Continue downstream on smoother trail. Note the sizable hemlocks that grow in the gorge. The evergreen shrub growing on some of the boulders is American yew.

At 1.0 km (0.6 mile) you arrive at McConnells Mill. In the 19th century this wild and rugged location was valued not for its beauty but for its energy. When Thomas McConnell modernized his newly purchased mill in 1875, water power was still holding its own against steam. The mill was run by turbines rather than a waterwheel, making it one of the most modern in the century. This mill is still in operating order and on occasion is opened to the public. The mill and adjacent property were obtained by the Western Pennsylvania Conservancy and later conveyed to the state.

Just beyond the mill is a covered bridge dating from 1874. You will return across this bridge, so pass it by for now, and continue on the self-guiding Kildoo Nature Trail. The Kildoo Trail is paved! Enjoy it while you can, for there is plenty of rough trail ahead with rocks and mud. Signs here bear the logo of the North Country National Scenic Trail. When completed, the North Country Trail will run from New York State to North Dakota.

McConnells was not the only mill to use Slippery Rock Creek. At post 7 look for the ruins of another mill. At 1.4 km (0.9 mile) you cross a footbridge over Kildoo Creek. Here you leave the pavement behind and continue on rough trail. Keep watch just beyond here for millstones from an abandoned gristmill.

You reach the Eckert Bridge at 2.7 km (1.7 miles). The road is gated off at the west end of the Eckert Bridge. Cross this bridge, and turn right at the far side on the return trail. Note the millstone mounted on a pedestal just beyond the bridge. By far the largest part of McConnells Mill State Park lies downstream from the Eckert Bridge. In the '90s a trail was built along Slippery Rock Creek and up Hells Hollow by the Keystone Trails Association, Shenango Outing Club, and other volunteer organizations (see Hike 42). The North Country Trail continues downstream to Hells Hollow.

Moving upstream, you pass repeated displays of white and red trillium in season. Elsewhere trilliums are rare, but when conditions are right, they can be locally abundant. This trail is much less used than the Kildoo, and you may well experience moments when you seem to be alone in the gorge.

At 4.3 km (2.7 miles) you turn right and wait your chance to cross the covered bridge. Auto traffic is one way at a time on the bridge, and you may have to take the bridge on the run when the traffic changes direction. This brings you back to the mill for one last look and a drink at the fountain.

If the traffic is very light, follow the road back to the parking lot. It's an easy climb and passes between house-sized blocks of sandstone. If traffic is at its usual heavy level, head upstream along the trail, and at 5.0 km (3.1 miles) turn right at the sign to the parking lot. The climb is steep but short, and you are soon back to your car.

Other attractions in McConnells Mill State Park are Cleland Rock and Hells Hollow Trail. Cleland Rock provides views of Slippery Rock Gorge and is reached from Breakneck Bridge Road. Hells Hollow Trail leads to a waterfall and an old iron furnace and is located on the west side of the park.

39

Glacier Ridge Trail

Distance: *7.6 km (4.7 miles)*

Time: *2½ hours*

Rise: *80 meters (260 feet)*

Highlights: *North Country National Scenic Trail; view*

Maps: *USGS 7½' Prospect, Slippery Rock; park map*

This section of the Glacier Ridge Trail follows a corridor of state park land along PA 528 that was purchased with the express intention of connecting Moraine State Park and Jennings Environmental Education Center with a foot trail. The Glacier Ridge Trail has since been designated as a portion of the North Country National Scenic Trail. Such foresight does not always prevail. Moraine State Park is not connected with nearby McConnells Mill State Park.

This is a car shuttle hike. First drive to Jennings Environmental Education Center at the junction of PA 8, PA 173, and PA 528—the same trailhead as Hike 34. Park one car here in either of the lots at Jennings. Then drive south on PA 528 for 3.2 miles, and park along the road opposite the road leading to a boat launch area. Walking shoes should be fine for this short hike, although there are some wet spots.

Follow the obvious path to the left of the road to the boat launch. The trail is marked with blue blazes. Pass a trail register, and then cross a bridge. Bear right after 100 meters (about 330 feet) on the trail relocation of September 1998, cut by a joint trail care of the Butler Outdoor Club and Keystone Trails Association. The meadow you are crossing is an old strip mine that is revegetating on its own. Then turn right and climb on sidehill construction. Next, turn right again, and proceed along the top of the old strip mine to 0.6 km (0.4 mile) and a view of Lake Arthur.

Then turn left, and follow new trail along the top of the hill. Bear right on a pole line,

The view toward Moraine Park

and cross paved Barely Road at 2.1 km (1.3 miles).

Continue along the pole line, and pass several old apple trees. Few if any bear any apples, but such old orchards are good places to see a variety of birds. Cross a gravel road at 2.4 km (1.5 miles) and the paved West Liberty Road at 2.7 km (1.7 miles)—just to the left is PA 528. Continue along the pole line to 3.1 km (1.9 miles) where you bear right into the woods.

Cross a couple of old grades followed by a stream and then a dry streambed. At 3.8 km (2.3 miles) there's a junction with a mysterious yellow-blazed trail that goes to the right. This trail is not shown on any map.

Next, the trail enters an open area, which is another reclaimed strip mine. The mine has been planted to white pines that seem to be thriving so that in a few years there will be an abundance of trees to blaze as well as to shade your way. Near 4.5 km (2.9 miles) you again get a mowed path to follow. Pass through some red pines, and find some more blazes. The trail then follows the border of a marsh (formerly a pond) and crosses the outlet. Next, you pass a house

to the right and then some more red pines. The trail emerges at a gravel road but turns left into the woods without crossing.

Shortly beyond, at 5.3 km (3.3 miles) cross paved Staff Road. Climb the bank, and continue through a patch of young sassafras trees.

Turn right on new trail at 6.4 km (4.0 miles). The old trail continues ahead but is now white-blazed. This is another part of the relocations of September 1998. Next, turn left on the Ridge Trail, and cross a pole line. At 7.1 km (4.4 miles) cross a bridge, and turn left on Black Cherry Trail, still following the blue blazes.

Turn left, and cross Big Run on a footbridge at 7.3 km (4.5 miles). Continue on Old Elm Trail to the picnic Area at Jennings. Then turn left to reach the parking lot.

A nearby hiking opportunity is Hike 34, which takes you on a tour of the prairie and other habitats at Jennings.

How is the North Country Trail to proceed from here? It will cross PA 8 and proceed through woods in back of the Old Stone House and then follow roads to State Game Land No. 95.

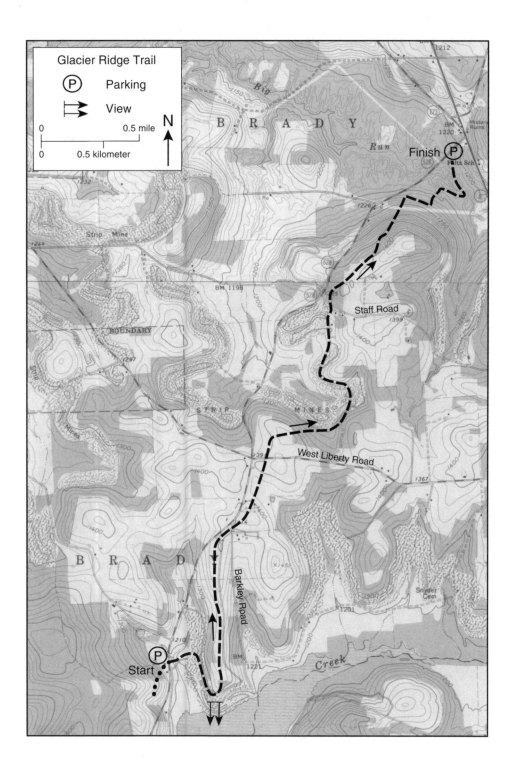

Glacier Ridge Trail

P   Parking

⊢→   View

0   0.5 mile

0   0.5 kilometer

N

B R A D Y

Big

Run

Finish P

Staff Road

West Liberty Road

Barkley Road

Snyder Cem

B R A D

Start
P

STRIP MINES

Creek

40

Hidden River Bridge

Distance: 7.4 km (4.6 miles)

Time: 2¾ hours

Rise: 80 meters (260 feet)

Highlights: Glacier Ridge Trail; Hidden River Bridge

Maps: USGS 7½' Prospect, Portersville; park map

Moraine State Park is located about 1 hour north of Pittsburgh at the junction of I-79 and US 422. Glacial Lakes Arthur and Edmund just to the north were formed when the continental glacier blocked the valleys of Slippery Rock and Muddy Creek. A dam on Muddy Creek recreates Lake Arthur, although the original lake was considerably higher and about 10 kilometers (6 miles) longer. The terminal moraines of the Illinoisan Ice Sheet and two major advances of the Wisconsin Glacier are located just to the north and west of Moraine State Park. Before the park could be opened to the public, over 400 abandoned oil, gas, and water wells had to be plugged to stop seepage that would have polluted the lake.

Most recreational opportunities at Moraine utilize Lake Arthur, but the northern shore has an attraction for hikers in the Glacier Ridge Trail. This trail currently extends from the west end of Lake Arthur to Jennings Environmental Education Center on PA 8. The Glacier Ridge Trail has been designated as part of the North Country National Scenic Trail, which is to extend over 5,000 kilometers (3,100 miles) from Crown Point in New York to the Missouri River in North Dakota. Another segment of the North Country Trail is in McConnells Mill State Park on Slippery Rock Creek. The two parks are connected by 4 kilometers (2.5 miles) of road walking. This hike on the Glacier Ridge Trail replaces one just to the east, which has been degraded by the proximity of a mountain bike trail.

To reach the trailhead for this car shuttle hike, take exit 99 from I-79, and head east

Hidden River Bridge

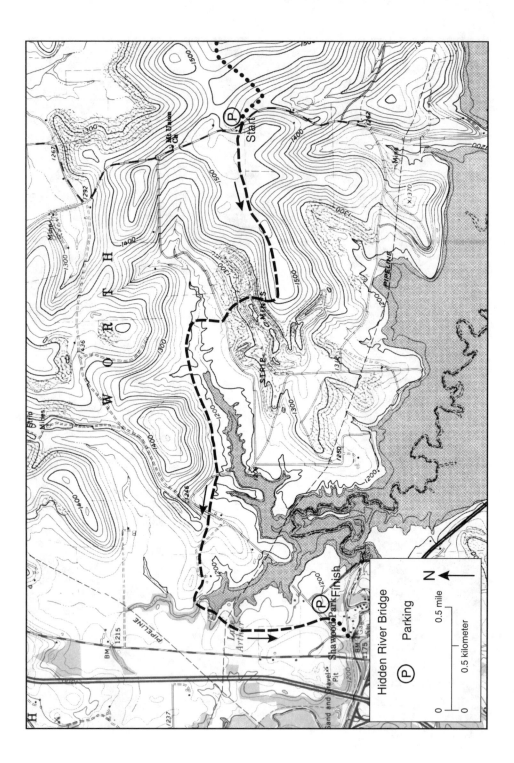

Hidden River Bridge

(P) Parking

N

0   0.5 kilometer

0   0.5 mile

on US 422. There is no access to the North Shore from PA 422 east, so continue east on PA 422 for about 2.5 miles, and take the South Shore exit. Get onto PA 422 west here, and take the North Shore exit. Drive about 0.2 mile, crossing Muddy Creek, and turn right to McDanel's boat launch. McDanel's can also be reached from the North Shore and West Park Roads. Leave one car at McDanel's, and turn right on North Shore Drive. Continue past the concession for the paved bicycle path and Watts Bay Marina for 5.3 miles. Just after the one-way section, turn left at a road junction. This is Mt. Union Road, but there isn't any sign. Drive 0.2 mile to the crossing of the Glacier Ridge Trail. Park on the right where there is space for several cars.

To start your hike, cross the road and climb on the blue-blazed trail, passing a water tower to the left. Soon you reach the top of the hill. Continue through a good stand of timber—tulip trees, red maples, and oaks. A field is visible to the right, apparently on private land.

The trail continues on an old woods road. Next, the trail descends and reaches a large steel water tank at 1.8 km (1.1 miles). Follow the blazes carefully here because the trail takes two right turns to get around the tank. There is a view to the left down the power line. The trail descends through an evergreen plantation, mostly white pines but an occasional red pine or spruce.

At 2.5 km (1.6 miles) jog right on an old road, crossing a stream. The trail continues through the evergreen plantation. At the bottom of the hill cross an old road and a pole line. Then cross a stream on a bridge.

Black cherry grows here. Climb past dead crab apple trees that show this is an old field returning to forest. Note the shagbark hickories. A field is visible to the left, and North Shore Drive can be seen. Turn right at the edge of the field, and continue through a larch plantation. Cross another bridge at 3.8 km (2.4 miles) and climb. The climb continues intermittently for some distance. At 4.9 km (3.0 miles) cross a gravel road with concrete steps on both sides. Then descend through another evergreen plantation. The trail then parallels a meadow before finally turning to cross it. At the far side the trail divides. The right fork proceeds to a parking area on North Shore Drive. Take the left fork, and cross North Shore drive at 5.6 km (3.5 miles).

Cross the paved bike trail (not to be confused with the Gnarly mountain bike trail) at 5.9 km (3.7 miles) and proceed to Hidden River Bridge, which was built by the Butler County Chapter of the North Country Trail Association and the Butler Outdoor Club. Then reach a trail register, and emerge behind the bicycle concession.

Turn left and follow a wide graveled path. Pass an out-of-commission drinking fountain and then a butterfly trail, both on the left. Pass a spruce plantation, and then turn left on the road to McDanel's boat launch to reach the parking lot at this trailhead.

Additional hiking opportunities at Moraine are the Glacier Ridge Trail along PA 528 (Hike 39) and the Sunken Garden, Wyggeston, and Hilltop Trails on the south shore. There are also trails at nearby McConnells Mill State Park (see Hikes 38 and 42).

41

Ryerson Station State Park

Distance: 8.6 km (5.3 miles)

Time: 3 hours

Rise: 240 meters (800 feet)

Highlight: Ryerson Lake

Maps: USGS 7½' Wind Ridge; state park map

Ryerson Station State Park consists of only 471 hectares (1,165 acres) on the north branch of the Dunkard Fork of Wheeling Creek in Greene County, a few kilometers from the West Virginia line. It's named after Fort Ryerson, built nearby in 1792 by order of Virginia authorities. The fort was a place of refuge for settlers during Indian raids.

Ryerson State Park can be reached from PA 21 about 22 miles west of I-79 or from PA 18 about 9 miles from Holbrook. From PA 21 turn east on SR 3022 for 0.8 mile, and then turn right, crossing the ford below the Ryerson Lake dam. Continue for 0.7 mile to the large parking area that serves the picnic area and trailhead. Ordinary walking shoes are suitable for this hike.

Start to the right of the map board at the trailhead. Move into the woods on the Fox Feather Trail, and shortly turn right on the Lazear Trail. Named after a former land-owner, the Lazear Trail passes through some spruce plantings. At 0.5 km (0.3 mile) you pass a "wolf tree" to the right of the trail. This white oak, thought to be 300 years old, grew wide, spreading branches that now shade out trees underneath—thus it wolfs down the sunlight. This eliminates the competition but doesn't produce much saw timber. "Wolf tree" is an expression used by foresters.

Soon you also pass some poison ivy. Note the furry or hairy appearance of this well-established vine, which can help you to identify poison ivy even in winter.

At 0.8 km (0.5 mile) the Orchard Trail diverges left, but you bear right, passing a

The wolf tree

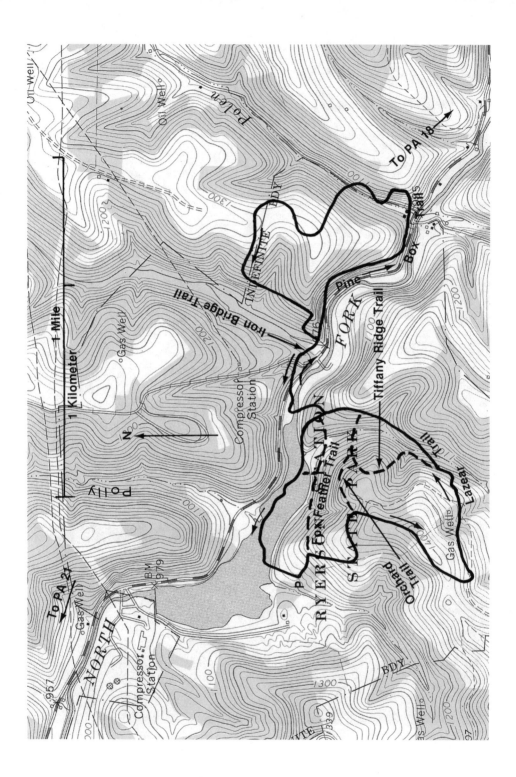

shagbark hickory. The top of the hill is reached at 1.3 km (0.8 mile) and provides a view of the lake more than 120 meters below.

Continuing on the Lazear Trail, you pass through a small meadow with more poison ivy before the trail descends into Mennell Hollow. Along the way you pass a sycamore wolf tree. The Tiffany Ridge Trail diverges to the left at 2.3 km (1.4 miles). The trails on this hill are liberally provided with benches should you decide to sit down to rest or contemplate.

The Tiffany Ridge Trail rejoins the Lazear Trail at 2.8 km (1.7 miles) as does the Fox Feather shortly beyond. At 3.1 km (1.9 miles) you turn right on the Iron Bridge Trail, cross the stream in the bottom of the hollow, and soon emerge along the edge of Ryerson Lake. Occasional bass croaks from the bottom of the bank announce the presence of bullfrogs. The Iron Bridge itself is reached at 3.7 km (2.3 miles). It once served a road across the North Fork but now carries only foot traffic. You will cross it on your way back, so pass it by for now and continue on the Pine Box Trail along the water's edge.

Ignore a swath to the right, and at 4.3 km (2.7 miles) climb the stream bank and shortly after emerge into a field. At 4.7 km (2.9 miles) turn left on the road, and cross a bridge over the North Fork to reach SR 3022. Cross this paved road, and bear left on the Pine Box Trail. Continue up the hill to 5.3 km (3.3 miles), where the trail leads ahead to the Stahl Cemetery. Now you see the origin of the Pine Box Trail. More than 40 people came up this hill in pine boxes. Curiously, there aren't any Stahls in the Stahl Cemetery; mostly, the residents are named Chess or Parson.

Back on the Pine Box Trail, you continue around the side of the hill along the contour before descending along the edge of a ravine that contains some large oak. At the bottom of Applegate Hollow you bear left and reach SR 3022 at 6.8 km (4.3 miles). Turn right on the road, cross the Iron Bridge, retrace your route on the Iron Bridge Trail, and then turn right on the Lazear Trail. At 7.8 km (4.9 miles) there's a view of the lake. Keep right, and you'll come out at its edge. Next, cross a bridge to the lake and follow the trail cut into the hillside. This brings you to a confusing four-way trail junction at 8.1 km (5.0 miles). Turn right to return to the lakeshore. Pass behind the boat-rental hut, and bear left through the picnic area past a drinking fountain and rest rooms to the parking lot.

There are other hikes in Ryerson Station State Park on the Three Mitten, Polly Hollow, Iron Bridge, and Deer Trails north of the lake. Enlow Fork (Hike 43) is also in Greene County.

42

Slippery Rock Gorge Trail

Distance: 9.9 km (6.1 miles)

Time: 4½ hours

Rise: 245 meters (800 feet)

Highlights: Wildflowers; wild gorge; big trees

Maps: USGS 7½' Portersville; park map

This portion of the North Country National Scenic Trail is the result of a campfire at Tamarack Fire Tower in Sproul State Forest in August 1990. Sitting around the campfire, members of Keystone Trails Trail Care Team discussed the difficulties we had in finding significant trail projects in the western part of the state. We decided to build a trail through the inaccessible part of McConnells Mill State Park from Eckert Bridge to Hell's Hollow. There already was a corridor of state park land down Slippery Rock Creek and up Hell Run.

Under the leadership of the Shenango Outing Club and several people in the Pittsburgh area, the project took off. A route was explored, flagged, and approved. The first work trip started in from Hell's Hollow in September 1991. A great deal of sidehill construction was required. Sidehill work is done with a tool called a Pulaski. Named for a forester, a Pulaski consists of an ax blade on one side and a hoe or adz on the other at the end of a pick handle. The hoe is used to dig away the ground until a root is struck, and then the ax blade is used to chop through the root.

After three years of work the resulting trail is not an easy one. The Gorge Trail was formally opened on April 30, 1994. Apart from several serious climbs there is a lot of up and down along the way. At places the footway is narrow, and you must watch your footing to avoid stepping off onto steep slopes. Wear your hiking boots for their added traction and against the many seeps and wet spots along the way.

Slippery Rock Creek

Slippery Rock Gorge was created in the last ice age when glacial Lake Arthur found a new outlet here. The enormous flow of meltwater cut this gorge in only a few thousand years. Consequently, the gorge is still changing even on our human time scale, as several recent landslides show.

The different rock layers contribute to a variety of soils, and the many seeps mean that wet and dry sites alternate along the trail. At least 69 species of wildflowers have been identified, making spring an excellent time to take this hike. The colors of fall make that season a strong second choice, but the Gorge Trail should be avoided in winter when ice may lurk beneath a veneer of snow. Wildflowers include white and red trillium, jack-in-the-pulpit, wild azalea, mayapple, and blue phlox.

This is *not* a circuit hike—it requires a car shuttle—and it should not be your first hike. From exit 96 on I-79, drive west on PA 488 through Portersville for a total of 4.3 miles. Then turn right on Heinz Camp Road for 4.7 miles, crossing Slippery Rock Creek on the Armstrong Bridge. Lastly, turn right on Shaffer Road for just 0.1 mile to Hell's Hollow Falls parking lot. Leave one car here.

To reach Eckert Bridge and the start of this hike, turn right on Shaffer Road. After 0.5 mile, turn right on Fairview School Road. Follow this road for 2.6 miles, and turn right on McConnells Mill Road, which you follow for 2.0 miles, and cross Slippery Rock Creek on the covered bridge. Then turn right on a dirt road that takes you up the side of the valley. Continue ahead at the top of the hill to Cheeseman Road. Turn right and follow Cheeseman Road downhill past a partial barricade to Eckert Bridge. Park here and begin your hike at the far side of Slippery Rock Creek.

Your hike starts at an old millstone mounted on a pedestal. Rectangular blue

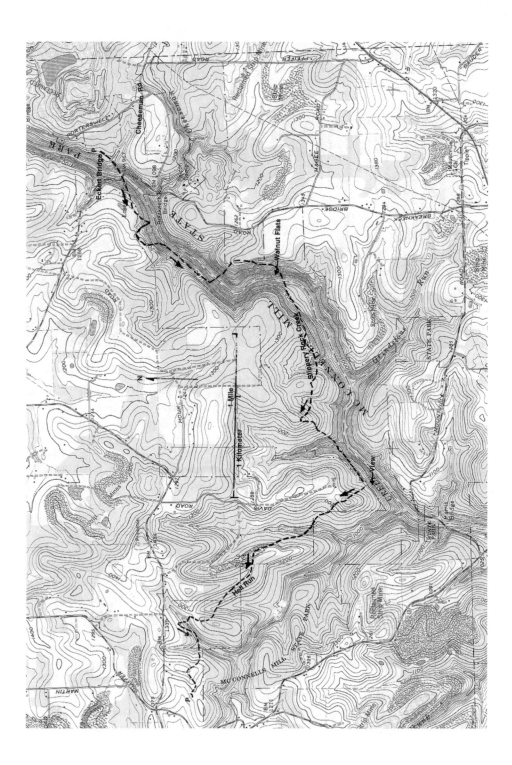

paint blazes mark the trail. This hike is laid out so as to do the hardest part of the Gorge Trail first. There is a fair amount of poison ivy along this first section. The trail is rocky and has lots of ups and downs. It closely follows Slippery Rock Creek, affording you a chance to watch kayaks if the water level is high enough. Across the creek you can see where Breakneck Run enters.

Soon you cross the first of many seeps. The trail climbs above the creek level only to return again several times. At 1.0 km (0.6 mile) it turns right and climbs steeply through a hemlock grove. At 1.1 km (0.7 mile) the hardest part is over, and the trail proceeds through fairly open woods, crossing a couple of side streams.

At 1.7 km (1.1 miles) the cliffs close in from the right and the trail continues along a bench. You pass above a fairly recent landslide at 2.0 km (1.3 miles) and shortly you cross a 1983 slide. Black birch, red maple, and sumac are now growing on this slide.

Next, the trail descends steeply on switchbacks and crosses still another landslide—this one from 1990—at the bottom. At 3.4 km (2.1 miles) you reach Walnut Flats, a level area in the midst of the gorge. You are back at creek level.

You are now entering the most remote portion of the Gorge Trail. Cross a stream, and then climb to a bench above the creek. It is this bench that makes the Gorge Trail possible. You cross a series of gullies cut by side streams. The steepness of the valley walls made logging difficult to impossible, so some old-growth oaks, beeches, hemlocks, basswoods, and maples survive along stretches of the trail. Blowdowns are nearly a meter in diameter and are difficult to clear even with a chainsaw. Sometimes the trail is

simply rerouted around a blowdown. Listen to the wind in the trees and the sounds of the creek below. This is the way it was some three centuries ago from the lakes to the sea.

At 6.0 km (3.8 miles) you reach an unblazed but obvious side trail on the left to where Hell Run enters Slippery Rock Creek. Descend for a last view of the creek and small waterfalls on Hell Run. On returning, turn up Hell Run to a side stream, and cross a horse path. Beyond the stream, bear right and then turn left, climbing to the edge of the valley above Hell Run.

Cross a natural bridge at 7.3 km (4.6 miles). Here a side stream has dissolved the limestone underneath the trail. At 7.6 km (4.7 miles) there's another natural bridge, followed shortly by a hemlock glen.

Next, cross another stream and climb still higher. Chestnut oaks and mountain laurels grow here as do wild azaleas. At 8.4 km (5.2 miles) the trail skirts a corner of private land. The border is marked with white blazes. At several places these boundaries, rather than the lay of the land, determine the trail route. The trail next descends, crossing a foot-bridge at 8.9 km (5.5 miles). The trail here shows signs of heavy use. After returning to Hell Run, you cross three more bridges over seeps and side streams to reach a junction with the main but unblazed Hell Hollow Trail. Turn right and cross Hell Run on a foot-bridge to the parking lot and the car you left there.

Another hiking opportunity at McConnells Mill is Hike 38, which could be combined with this hike, at least in part. Hikes 39 and 40 are found at nearly Moraine State Park, and Hike 34, at Jennings Environmental Education Center, is just a bit farther.

43

Enlow Fork

In-and-out distance: 10.6 km (6.6 miles)

Time: 3 hours

Rise: 85 meters (280 feet)

Highlight: Wildflowers

Maps: USGS 7½' Wind Ridge

By means of a cooperative effort involving two public agencies, a large corporation, and the Western Pennsylvania Conservancy, the 405-hectare Enlow Fork Natural Area has been permanently protected as State Game Land No. 302. The Enlow Fork of Wheeling Creek forms the boundary between Greene and Washington counties near the West Virginia line. This hike is an easy one with special rewards for birders and all who like wildflowers. Along the Enlow Fork the ranges of southern and western plants and trees overlap the ranges of plants and trees more familiar to Pennsylvanians. The hike follows an old dirt road now closed to traffic along the bottom lands bordering the Enlow Fork. It is an in-and-out hike so it can be truncated anywhere by just retracing your footsteps.

The trailhead is deep in the hills and hollows of southwestern Pennsylvania. Take exit 6 from I-70 at Claysville, and turn right (east) onto US 40. After 0.9 mile turn right (south) onto PA 231. Follow PA 231 for 3.5 miles and bear right onto SR 3029 to West Finley, where PA 231 starts downhill. Continue for 7.9 miles to the junction in West Finley, and turn left onto SR 3037. Follow this road for 2.4 miles and turn sharp right over an iron bridge at Burdette onto Walker Hill Road. Follow this gravel road uphill for 1.7 miles, and turn very sharply right (more than 90 degrees) onto Smoky Row Lane, another gravel road. A sign at this junction says STATE GAME LAND. Follow this road for 1.2 miles downhill, and park in a field on your left just before you come to a gate across

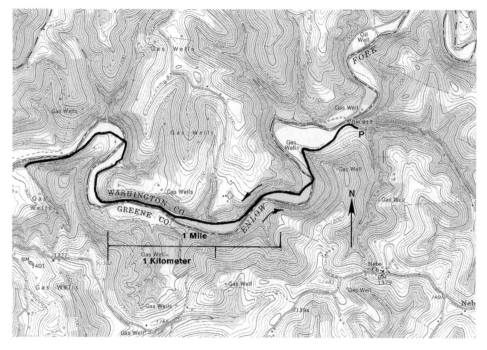

this road. Despite the length of this hike and some wet spots, ordinary walking shoes should be adequate.

To start the hike, squeeze around the gate, and follow the dirt road past the stone abutments of an old bridge across Enlow Fork. Next, you will come to an extensive meadow that is an old corn field. The Game Commission management plan calls for maintaining these fields by mowing them.

At 0.7 km (0.4 mile) the old road turns sharply to the south. Look on your right for the chinquapin or yellow oak. It resembles chestnut oak, but its leaves are white and hairy underneath, and it rarely grows to tree size.

At 1.1 km (0.7 mile) you cross an iron bridge over Enlow Fork. Look for a giant sycamore on your left. In May you will also find hectares of blue-eyed Mary and Virginia bellflower along this part of the trail. Blue-eyed Mary is a plant of the Midwest and is rarely found in Pennsylvania.

Birds found along the Enlow Fork are indigo bunting, scarlet tanager, pileated woodpecker, downy woodpecker, belted kingfisher, and yellow-throated warbler.

At 2.1 km (1.3 miles) and 2.3 km (1.4 miles) roads enter from the right. There is a giant elm tree on the left just past the second road. Goldenrod is found in abundance.

At 2.5 km (1.5 miles) you pass another iron bridge on your left and continue down the dirt road. At 4.0 km (2.5 miles) you cross still another iron bridge. Look for flood debris on the deck of this bridge, and as the road climbs above the stream, look for a beaver dam. Where the road turns sharply to the left, look for old beaver cuttings. There is a cliff farther down on this side. Why did the beaver climb way up here to cut trees when there are plenty of trees next to the stream on the other side?

At 5.2 km (3.2 miles) you come into view of a flood control dam to your right. The dam has an opening at its base that allows the stream

Crossing Enlow Fork on a steel truss bridge

to pass through. In times of flood, the excess water is held temporarily behind the dam and only the normal flow continues downstream.

Just beyond there is another gate across the road. Turn back and retrace your steps to your car.

Other hiking opportunities in south western Pennsylvania are at Ryerson Station State Park (Hike 41).

44

Raccoon Creek State Park

Distance: 13.3 km (8.3 miles)

Time: 4¾ hours

Rise: 240 meters (780 feet)

Highlights: Small lake; pleasant walk in the woods

Maps: USGS 7½' Hookstown; park map

Raccoon Creek State Park is one of the five mini national parks established in Pennsylvania by the National Park Service during the Great Depression. The Works Progress Administration (WPA) and Civilian Conservation Corps (CCC) built many of the recreational facilities. All five parks were transferred to the commonwealth in 1945. Since then, the state has built the large lake (1948), swimming and picnic area (1950), and family campground (1956).

Raccoon Creek Park is large by Pennsylvania standards—2,963 hectares (7,319 acres). Despite its name, the park is mostly in the valley of Traverse Creek. The Park is 25 miles west of Pittsburgh and can be reached from US 30 at the east end. PA 18 passes directly through, and PA 168 grazes the west end of the park.

I hesitate to recommend the park map as a trail map. It has trails that start and end in the middle of the woods, and it omits vital trail segments and old roads that are essential for hiking. Raccoon Creek State Park needs a trail inventory. Since hikers are the most invisible of all park users, trail work in state parks is usually up to volunteers from the hiking community.

This hike is a substantial loop hike in the larger portion of the park west of PA 18. It's a varied hike, using streamside trails, upland trails, and roads closed to most traffic. Hiking boots and long pants are recommended because of the mud and briers. There is also some poison ivy along the way. Large parts of this hike are on multiuse trails open to horses but not bicycles.

A positive posting sign at Raccoon Creek State Park

To reach the trailhead, drive west from the park office on PA 18 for 0.9 mile, crossing Traverse Creek. Park just beyond in a small lot on the right. (This parking area is shown in the wrong place on the park map.)

To start, walk back over Traverse Creek, and turn left on a gated old road now called the Wetland Trail. At 0.5 km (0.3 mile) reach the spillway of a dam, built in the early 1950s, forming a small lake on Traverse Creek. The trail continues in the open along the side of the lake. At first the trail is mowed, but the briers close in beyond. At the far end the lake becomes a cattail marsh. Continue past a small beaver dam on Traverse Creek.

Cross a side stream in a culvert at 1.7 km (1.1 miles) and enter the forest, escaping the briers. Cross a small stream as best you can, and then bear left on Nichol Road at 2.1 km (1.3 miles). Take a good look at this

junction because you will have to find it on the way back, and it's marked only with a positive posting sign which indicates allowed uses. Nichol Road is open only to handicapped hunters and people using the Pioneer primitive campsite in the west end of the park. Traverse Creek can be seen flowing freely on the left.

A side road comes in, and you turn left, crossing a bridge over Traverse Creek at 2.7 km (1.7 miles). Just beyond, turn right on the Equestrian Trail. Raccoon Creek State Park uses a form of positive posting, and a sign is posted at each trail with decals showing the permitted uses. The Wetland Trail is open only to hikers, while the Equestrian Trail is also open to hiking and cross country skiing. The Equestrian Trail is yellow blazed and well used, but watch your step to avoid "road apples." There is a trail register at this junction.

Climb out of the valley on switchbacks, and continue through open woods featuring oaks, black cherry, and shagbark hickory. Note that on the Equestrian Trail blow-downs are not removed but detoured. Thus the trail becomes more twisting with each new blowdown. A passing thought: When the old blowdowns finally rot away does the trail ever return to the original route? No. Brush and saplings will have grown up.

Reach the top of the hill at 3.4 km (2.1 miles) and at 4.0 km (2.5 miles) cross the boundary of a no-hunting area surrounding the Pioneer primitive campsite. Most of the park is open to hunting during the regular seasons. Pass a side trail to the left at 4.2 km (2.6 miles) that presumably leads to the Pioneer area and then continue out of the no-hunting area. Black gum, maple, cucumber (actually a magnolia), and tulip poplar add to the forest diversity.

At 5.6 km (3.5 miles) ignore a trail from the right that presumably leads to a paved

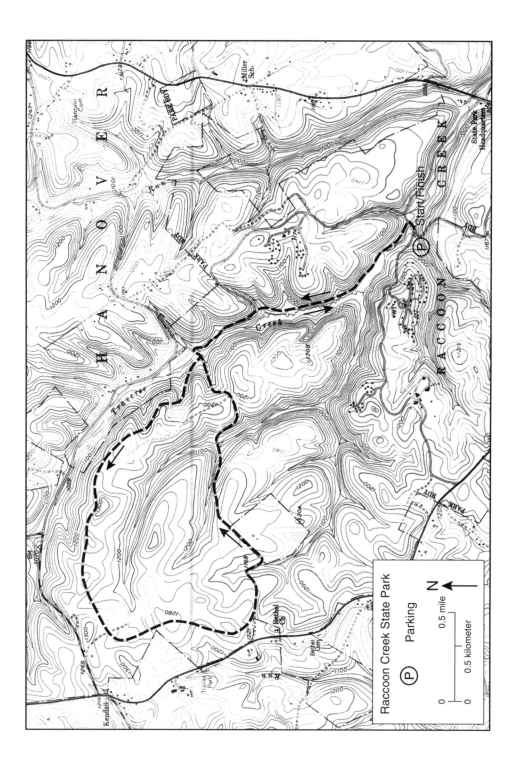

Raccoon Creek State Park

Ⓟ Parking

N

0   0.5 mile
0   0.5 kilometer

road along Traverse Creek. This intersection is complicated by another detour around a blowdown. Next, cross the bed of an intermittent stream, and pass a large sycamore to the right of the trail. The sycamore is largely rotted out at the base, and someday soon it will fall across the trail, causing an extensive detour. An old fence line comes in from the right, a relic of the submarginal farmlands that were bought up to form this park back in the Great Depression. The ruins of an old springhouse are to the left. Reach the top of a hill at 6.5 km (4.0 miles).

At 7.6 km (4.7 miles) turn left on Nichol Road. It appears to have been rerouted to avoid adjacent private land. At 8.1 km (5.0 miles) another equestrian trail, this one unblazed, turns off to the right. Then cross a bridge and climb to the edge of a large field on the right. Pass a number of roads to the left and right but continue ahead on Nichol Road, which is older than the others. Pass the far side of a field at 8.7 km (5.4 miles).

Next, pass a mighty oak on the left side of the road. If you look back, you will see that much of the main trunk is hollow. At 9.5 km (5.9 miles) cross two streams in culverts. An old beaver dam is just below on the second stream. Then climb another hill.

At the top a trail comes in from the right just before a vehicle gate. The road to the Pioneer tent area turns left at this point. From here on, Nichol Road is yellow blazed. The road descends gently to Traverse Creek. I found no trace of the trail indicated on the park map between the top of the hill and Traverse Creek. Close the loop at 10.6 km (6.6 miles).

Retrace your steps, remembering to turn right after the bridge, and then bear right on the Wetland Trail.

Additional hiking opportunities can be found at Raccoon Creek State Park on a system of trails at Frankfort Mineral Spring reached from a trailhead on PA 18, and in the Wildflower Reserve on US 30 at the east end of the park.

Allegheny Gorge

45

Presque Isle State Park

Distance: 6.3 km (3.9 miles)

Time: 2 hours

Rise: 3 meters (10 feet)

Highlights: Lake Erie; lighthouse

Maps: USGS 7½' Erie North; state park map

Presque Isle is a sandspit in the shallow waters of Lake Erie. To our eyes, it's part of the permanent landscape. But if we had taken time-lapse photographs over the past few hundred years, we would see that it is actually moving. Beaches on the western side are washed away, only to become new land on the eastern side. Under the action of wind and waves, the entire pile of sand has moved east about 800 meters in the past century. Coming from the mainland, you pass through several centuries of plant succession. First are oak, sugar maple, and hemlock—the climax vegetation. Then there are white pine, poplar, red maple, and cedar—sun-loving trees that provide shade for the shade-tolerant species that form the climax forest. Next, you leave the trees behind and reach an area covered with shrubs and other small plants. Finally, at the eastern tip, you find dunes and beaches that have just been formed. This new land is stabilized by young poplars whose roots anchor the moving sand.

Presque Isle has its share of human history, as well. Commodore Perry's fleet was built here during the War of 1812. After defeating the British, Perry's flotilla remained at Misery Bay for the rest of the war. A full-sized replica of Perry's flagship, the *Niagara,* is on display in downtown Erie.

To reach the park and trailhead from I-79, turn west on US 20 (26th Street), and then turn north on PA 832 (Peninsula Drive), which takes you out onto Presque Isle. At 1.5 miles beyond the park office, turn left and then right on Mill Road. Another 0.6 mile brings you to the trailhead

The Presque Isle lighthouse

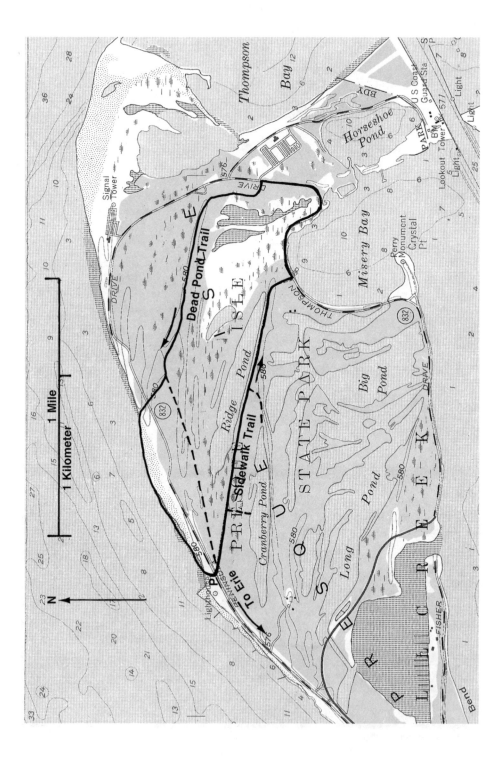

for the Sidewalk Trail. Park in a small lot at the Sidewalk trailhead or in another lot across the road. Ordinary walking shoes or sneakers are fine for this hike, but you will need some strong insect repellent. There is some poison ivy along the trail, but the trails are mowed so it's easily avoided. In the past, Presque Isle was a hot spot for Lyme disease, but controlled hunting has reduced the deer herd and the risk.

Presque Isle is a heavily used park, and on summer weekends it may be wall-to-wall people. The inside trails are the least-used facilities in the park, however, and you may find some solitude there even during peak visiting times.

In years when lake levels are high, the water table rises all over the peninsula, and some trails may be flooded, but the Sidewalk Trail is built up so it is most likely to remain open. Presque Isle uses a form of positive posting on trails: decals showing the permitted uses are displayed at the trailhead. The Sidewalk Trail is open to hiking and cross-country skiing.

To start, first you pass the end of the Dead Pond Trail, which comes in from the left, and then you pass the Marsh and Fox Trails that diverge to the right. Trees growing along this section are red oak, red maple, chokecherry, pin oak, ash, and willow. In the early days of the lighthouse, the Sidewalk Trail was the supply route for keepers at what was called the loneliest place on earth. The trail led to a boathouse on Misery Bay, and the keeper then rowed the rest of the way to town. The Sidewalk Trail was paved in 1925.

At 1.0 km (0.6 mile) you can see the open water of Ridge Pond to your left. The pond is a good habitat for ducks, and you may be able to hear them, even if you can't see them. There are also flocks of great blue herons. Serviceberry and chokecherry grow along this section. Both fruits are edible. The serviceberry is luscious when fresh; chokecherries are extremely tart and really pucker up your mouth.

Soon the Sidewalk Trail turns right and ends at Thompson Road on the edge of Misery Bay, where Perry's fleet was stationed. The Perry Monument can be seen across the bay. Turn left along Thompson Drive. Keep left, facing traffic, as you round the edge of Niagara Pond. Here you find poplars growing along the bay. On the far side of the pond you pass gray birch, jack pine, and pitch pine.

At 3.1 km (1.9 miles) turn left on the Dead Pond Trail. (If this trail is under water, retrace your steps to the Sidewalk Trail.) Deer tracks and coyote scat show that people are not the only ones using the trails. Like the Sidewalk Trail, this trail is mostly in the open, but whenever you pass through a patch of woods, the deer flies close in—most insect repellents don't seem to bother deer flies. Ignore the first trail to the right and a number of trails to the left, all unsigned.

At 4.6 km (2.9 miles) bear right on the B Trail, and it soon brings you out to Pine Tree Road. Cross the road, proceed to the beach, and bear left. Lake Erie is truly an inland sea. You can't see the other side. Erie and the other Great Lakes are the world's largest deposits of fresh water in the liquid state.

Continue along the beach until you approach the lighthouse. Built in 1872, the lighthouse isn't very high and just barely gets above the treetops. This is your landmark to turn inland, and you should come out on the road within sight of your car.

A paved multipurpose trail has been built along the bay side from the park entrance to Perry's monument, and it presents another hiking opportunity at Presque Isle State Park. But watch out for bicyclists and in-line skaters.

46

Oil Creek State Park

Distance: 8.5 km (5.3 miles)

Time: 3 hours

Rise: 290 meters (950 feet)

Highlight: Oil Creek Gorge

Maps: USGS 7½' Titusville South; park map

This hike takes you along historic and beautiful Oil Creek, south of Titusville. Oil seeps have occurred in this valley since prehistoric times. Indians dug pits to collect the oil. Here in 1859 "Colonel" Edwin Drake drilled the world's first oil well. By good fortune, Drake struck oil only 23 meters (75 feet) down. Most of the producing oil sand was 150 meters (500 feet) below the valley floor. But Drake's luck deserted him, and he died poor while others made fortunes along Oil Creek and at what is now the ghost town of Pithole, just to the east. Some wells still produce oil nearby, and one has produced continuously since 1861. Pennsylvania rocks hold on to their oil so tenaciously that some of the last producing wells on dry land may turn out to be not too far from here.

The oil boom of the 1860s produced much of the technology still in use today. From the North Slope of Alaska to the floor of the North Sea to the far reaches of Siberia, inventions made here in Pennsylvania are still in use.

Much of this historic region is now contained in Oil Creek State Park, which stretches from PA 8 north to the Drake Well Historic Site. Ironically, perhaps, two attractions of this park that commemorate the dawn of the Petroleum Age are a bicycle trail, between the Drake Well and the park headquarters, and the Gerard Hiking Trail.

The Gerard Trail makes a loop of about 58 kilometers (36 miles), crossing Oil Creek on the PA 8 bridge and on the road bridge at the Drake Oil Well Historic Site. The trail was in large part the retirement project of Ray Gerard of Titusville. Two overnight

The suspension bridge over Oil Creek

shelter areas have been built along the trail, permitting backpacks of up to 3 days. This hike makes a circuit on the northernmost part of the Oil Creek Trail, using a footbridge over Oil Creek paid for by the Western Pennsylvania Conservancy. The Oil Creek Trail is one of the best maintained trails in the state, thanks to the Over-the-Hill Gang, a group of retired people from the Titusville area who work on the trail once a week. I did not find a blowdown anywhere, and at two places I saw where this year's summer growth had been trimmed.

To reach the trailhead from US 8 in Titusville, turn east at the first stoplight on the south side of town, and follow Bloss Street for 1.0 mile to a parking lot next to Oil Creek. This parking lot also serves the bicycle trailhead, so it could be crowded.

To start your hike on the yellow-blazed Oil Creek Trail, walk across Oil Creek on a sidewalk attached to the bridge to the Drake Well Historic Site. Then cross the railroad tracks. Beware, the Oil Creek and Titusville Railroad operates excursion trains on this line from March through October. Turn right and start to climb. Shortly, you switchback to the left on an old road to Pithole, which is Pennsylvania's largest ghost town. At the next right turn there's a view of Titusville from a power line swath, which also provides you with two more views farther along. Pass a trail register, where you should sign in, and then cross the power line at 1.3 km (0.8 mile). This time you get a view across the Oil Creek valley.

Beyond the swath, you continue climbing through an area that burned in 1982 from a mismanaged trash fire. At 1.7 km (1.1 miles) ignore the line of yellow blazes and white blazes crossing the trail. These appear to be the boundaries of the Drake Well Historic Site and Oil Creek Park, respectively.

Note the many sassafras seedlings growing along the trail. Sassafras leaves look like mittens. Some have left thumbs,

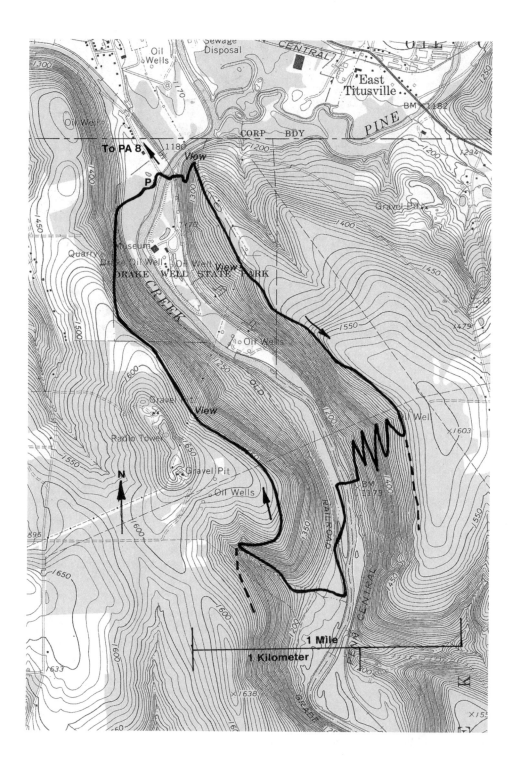

some have right thumbs, some have thumbs on both sides, and some have no thumbs at all. Sassafras leaves are highly variable and all shapes may be found on the same tree. Wild azaleas also grow here.

Cross an old pipeline swath at 2.7 km (1.7 miles) and bear right on a white-blazed connector trail. The connector trail switchbacks down the side of Oil Creek Gorge on a set of well-preserved old road grades. At 3.7 km (2.3 miles) cross the Oil Creek and Titusville Railroad tracks again and then the swinging bridge over Oil Creek that makes this hike possible. At the far side, turn left (downstream) at the edge of Oil Creek. Several old apple trees suggest that this was an orchard at one time.

The trail continues downstream on several old road grades, but at 4.5 km (2.9 miles) you turn right on a trail, passing an old wooden oil tank. Cross the paved bicycle trail, which follows an abandoned railroad grade, and continue across a clearing containing some ruins marking the historic site of Boughton. This was a sulfuric acid plant, and on some days you can still smell it.

This is one wound that nature has not been able to heal in over 100 years.

Continue climbing along a tiny run to 5.1 km (3.2 miles), where you turn right on the yellow-blazed West Side Trail. Switchback to the top of the hill, and cross an old pipeline swath at 6.0 km (3.7 miles). At 6.6 km (4.1 miles) cross the power line for a last view across Oil Creek. Soon the trail starts a gentle descent, passing oak trees over a meter in diameter. At 7.7 km (4.8 miles) pass another trail register. Be sure to sign in again. About 200 meters (650 feet) farther, turn right, cross the paved bicycle path, and descend steeply on steps. At the bottom are a bog bridge and an old steel oil tank. Note old pipes in the trail as you cross this bottomland. Soon you reach the edge of Oil Creek and head upstream to the parking lot.

There are plenty of additional hiking opportunities near Oil Creek State Park. Hike 48 offers a circuit hike starting from the park headquarters at Petroleum Center. And a flyer from the Western Pennsylvania Conservancy describes a 20 km (12.4 mile) 2-day backpack using the Drake Well trailhead.

47

Erie Extension Canal Towpath

In-and-out distance: 9.6 km (6.0 miles)

Time: 3 hours

Rise: 3 meters (10 feet)

Highlights: Pymatuning Swamp; waterfowl

Maps: USGS 7½' Conneaut Lake, Hartstown; Sportsman's Recreation map– State Game Lands No. 214

In the 1830s and '40s, Pennsylvania underwent a vast program of canal building. By the 1840s, canals stretched from the Delaware River to Lake Erie. These canals were not all built to the same standards. Locks on different canals were of various lengths and widths. Two rail links, the Columbia to Philadelphia Railroad in the east and the Allegheny Portage Railroad in the west, were also included. A great deal of loading and unloading was required, making the canal system uncompetitive with the fast-developing railroads. By the 1850s the railroads had gained the upper hand. While some canals continued in use until the 20th century, most were abandoned in the 19th. Most of the abandoned canals were bought by the very railroads they had competed with. Some were destroyed in the construction of railroads and highways, others by a century of floods and the growth of trees and other vegetation. Very few old canals, then, are found on public lands.

One part of the Erie Extension Canal and its towpath came into public ownership by accident, with the development of adjacent Pymatuning State Park. The Erie Extension Canal, completed in 1844, originally ran from the Ohio River up Beaver Valley to Erie, with a side canal down French Creek to the Allegheny River at Franklin. The canal crossed the backwaters of Pymatuning Swamp, and since the land was flat, no locks were required.

The canal towpath across the eastern arm of Pymatuning cut off a 240-hectare (600-acre) lake, which served as a reservoir for the canal. Canals used water every time

Open water in the old canal reservoir

a boat went through a lock, and the old canals probably lost a good deal of water through leakage, as well. If a canal ran out of water, the first boat to run aground blocked the channel and halted traffic in both directions.

The old towpath makes a very different sort of hike. There is no problem in following it. And while most trails require people to walk single file, this one is wide enough for two people to walk side by side. It's a good trail for a long talk with a friend. Unfortunately there is a considerable amount of illegal use by all-terrain vehicles.

A great many birds can be found along the trail. Chickadees chatter from the trees, herons stalk the shallows, kingfishers dart into the water, and a great honking over the swamp heralds the approach of a flight of geese. Don't forget your binoculars.

Although I expected insects to be a real problem, the hike is mostly out in the open,

and I didn't have to use repellent, even on a warm day in July. Almost any sort of shoes should be adequate for the excellent footway on this hike.

The trailhead is reached from US 322, 5.0 miles west of the junction with PA 18 in Conneaut Lake and just east of Hartstown. Turn north at the east side of the overpass that crosses the Bessemer and Lake Erie Railroad. This gravel road is very rough at first, so take it slow, and thread your way around the mud puddles at the bottom of the slope. Turn right at the bottom and continue. The cinder road swings away from the railroad, and at 1.0 mile from US 322 you reach a gate and the game commission parking lot. (This hike can also be done with a car shuttle that is obvious on the game lands map. Just drive back to US 322, and keep turning left until you reach PA 285. Then turn left again to a parking area on the left for a total of 5.5 miles.)

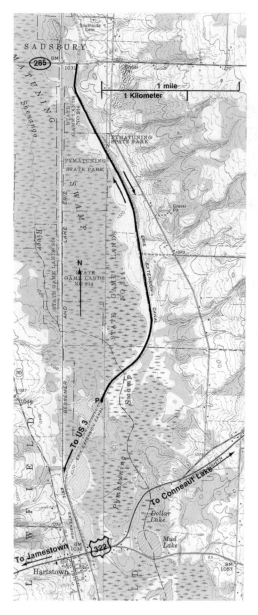

To start the hike, dodge around the gate, and head out along the old towpath. Note the difference in water levels on the two sides of the towpath. The water on the right is about two meters higher than the water on the left.

Trees along your route are chokecherry, aspen, red maple, elm, cucumber, cottonwood, walnut, locust, red oak, white oak, hickory, sassafras, willow, and apple. Sumac also grows here, as do wild strawberry and poison ivy. Fortunately the game commission mows the route, so the poison ivy does not reach the path.

At 0.8 km (0.5 mile) you cross a bridge over the dam that controls the level of the old reservoir. Here you clearly see the difference in water levels. This is a favorite spot of fishermen. In the reservoir water lilies abound; on the other side of the towpath the ground alternates between marsh and woods. Look for deer tracks on the path. Once I turned around and found a doe following me.

At 2.4 km (1.5 miles) you reach the site of an old bridge over the canal. A couple of planks across the trickle now provide access for fishermen. At 2.9 km (1.8 miles) you see farms along the far side of the valley, and at 4.8 km (3.0 miles) you reach the vehicle gate next to PA 285. Along the way you have crossed an unmarked corner of Pymatuning State Park. Ahead, the old towpath continues across private land before returning to the route of the Bessemer and Lake Erie Railroad. Turn and retrace your steps along the towpath to your car.

48

Petroleum Center

Distance: 11.5 km (7.1 miles)

Time: 4¼ hours

Rise: 325 meters (1,070 feet)

Highlights: Waterfall; ghost town

Maps: USGS 7½' Titusville South; park map

Petroleum Center may not be the largest of Pennsylvania's ghost towns, but in its heyday the town was certainly one of the wickedest. It was so named because it was in the center of the original oil region in the 1860s, halfway between Titusville and Oil City. Within 20 years the oil boom had moved on, and Petroleum Center was on its way to being a ghost town—but it had a lively time in between. President Ulysses S. Grant visited it in 1871, and on ordinary days a riot, fire, or shooting could happen at any minute, and there were shouts of new oil strikes or gushers; wild card games and brawls featured participants covered with mud and oil.

This circuit hike visits Petroleum Center and other petroleum-age sites along the Gerard Trail in Oil Creek State Park, and the woods are filled with ruins from this era. Roots across the trail may on closer inspection turn out to be steel pipes or rods.

The hike is entirely within the boundaries of Oil Creek State Park, which is one of five state parks established through the efforts of the Western Pennsylvania Conservancy.

The trailhead is at the headquarters for Oil Creek State Park. Drive up PA 8, and take the Oil City bypass. Then 1.0 mile beyond Rouseville turn right immediately after the PA 8 bridge over Oil Creek. Pass the ice control structure in the creek, and after 3.0 miles turn right, and cross Oil Creek on a steel bridge. After another 0.3 mile turn left for the parking lot at the park office. Because of many rocks and wet spots, you will want your hiking boots for this hike. Due to some very steep drop-offs

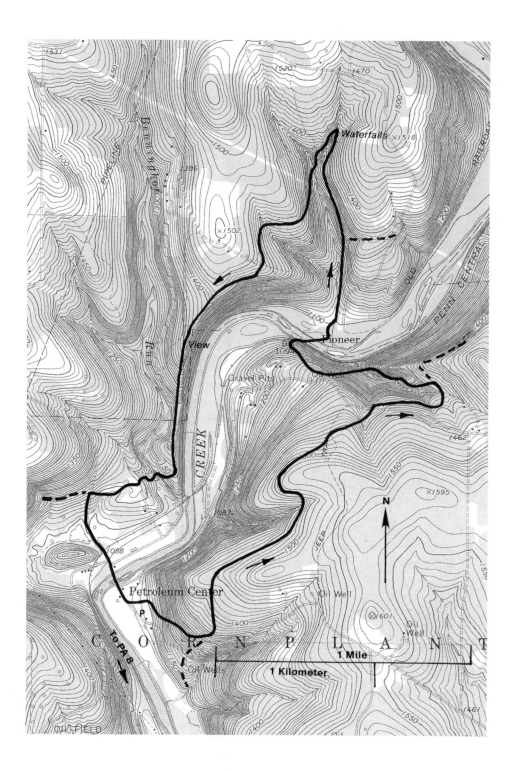

Waterfalls ×1518

Pioneer

View

Gravel Pits

CREEK

Petroleum Center

N

N 1595

×1601

Oil Well

Oil Well

To PA 8

OILFIELD

PENN CENTRAL

RAILROAD

1 Mile

1 Kilometer

along the connector trail this hike is not suitable for small children.

The start of the hike is marked by a HIKING TRAIL sign to the right of the park office. Head into the woods along the white blazes. Note the steel rods used to support the logs along the side of the trail. They are not steel rebar as is used on most trails but portions of the rods used to pump oil wells from a centrally located engine. If you look carefully you'll see how the rods were screwed together. Many tons of such rods were used to pump the wells along Oil Creek.

Just after crossing a pole line you reach the junction with the yellow-blazed main Oil Creek Trail at 0.5 km (0.3 mile). Turn left, and continue climbing among large boulders, recrossing the pole line. At the top of the climb you reach the edge of the Oil Creek Valley. The trail divides the hemlocks growing on the slope to your left and the deciduous trees growing on the level to your right. This is a particularly delightful section of trail.

The generally good condition of the Gerard Trail is due to the Over-the-Hill Gang. This group of retired people from the Titusville area gets together one day a week to work on the trail. The result is the blazes are freshly painted, there are signs at every junction, and most blowdowns are quickly removed.

A red-blazed cross-country ski trail comes in from the right at 1.4 km (0.9 mile) and continues along the Oil Creek Trail. The damage caused by tornadoes that struck western Pennsylvania on May 31, 1985 is no longer readily apparent. Today all you can see is that there are a lot of young trees, particularly black birch. Next, cross a bridge, and then come to a scenic overlook complete with bench above Oil Creek.

There's a trailside shelter at a trail junction at 2.8 km (1.8 miles). Bear left on the yellow-blazed trail, and ignore the white-blazed ski trail that diverges to the right. The trail descends, and you cross a power line. Cross Hemlock Road at 3.2 km (2.0 miles).

After crossing the headwaters of Hemlock Run and passing through some ruins, turn left on a white-blazed connector trail at 4.2 km (2.6 miles). Descend above Hemlock Run, first on a nice old grade and then on a trail next to a small pipeline. Cross Hemlock Run on a log bridge, and then climb steeply.

At the top, pass along the very edge of a steep drop to the Oil Creek and Titusville Railroad. Descend and cross the OC&TRR at 5.3 km (3.3 miles); then bear right on the paved bicycle trail and cross Oil Creek. Note that this bridge is built on the piers of a former railroad bridge. Immediately on the far side, bear left on the connector trail up Pioneer Run.

At 5.8 km (3.6 miles) a trail on the right leads to a parking lot at the end of Pioneer Road. Bear left and start the climb along Pioneer Run to the West Side Trail at 6.2 km (3.8 miles) and continue climbing gently along the yellow blazes. Cross another pole line, and then descend to Greg Falls at 6.8 km (4.2 miles). This is a very pretty spot and a good place for a break.

Back on the trail, cross Pioneer Run, and then turn downstream on the far side. In season look for trilliums. Descending, cross a tributary of Pioneer Run, and climb to an old grade that passes a shack dating from the oil-boom days. (When you get to the Drake Museum, look for the photo of Pioneer Run in the oil heyday. If the museum is closed, the same photo is on display at the McDonald's in Titusville.)

At 8.2 km (5.1 miles) turn left off an old road toward a metal shack that housed another oil well. There's a view to the left across Oil Creek at 8.6 km (5.3 miles) where

Oil Creek Trail

the trail crosses a former power line. Turn left off an old road, and proceed down a ridge between Benninghof Run and Oil Creek. Soon the trail enters an area of tornado damage and at a clearing continues on a logging road, passing another view of Oil Creek. At 10.2 km (6.3 miles) cross Benninghof Run on a highly arched bridge and a paved road (SR 1009). Continue through open woods and old fields, passing many ruins of the petroleum age. There is a long bridge over a wet area.

At 10.8 km (6.7 miles) turn left on a dirt road, which is actually the connector trail through Petroleum Center. Cross the Oil Creek and Titusville Railroad at the new depot, and enter downtown Petroleum Center. There are many interpretive signs along the walking tour of this ghost town. (For instance, Wildcat Hollow, just to the west of here, was named for a driller who shot a wildcat, stuffed it, and tied it to his derrick, so "wildcatting" became a term for all drillers who risked drilling in unproven territory.) At the center of town only the stone steps of the bank remain.

To complete the hike, walk across the steel bridge (one lane wide but two-way traffic), and make your way to the park office and its parking lot.

Other hiking opportunities at Oil Creek State Park include a circuit hike based at the Drake Well Historic Site. Other circuit hikes could be made by using the PA 8 bridge downstream or from the Miller Farm Historic Site upstream.

49

Allegheny Gorge

Distance: 11.7 km (7.3 miles)

Time: 4 hours

Rise: 310 meters (1,020 feet)

Highlights: Old iron furnace; view; mountain stream

Maps: USGS 7½' Kennerdell; state forest trail map for Allegheny Tract

In the 1970s the state purchased 1,280 hectares (3,160 acres) along the Allegheny River in Venango County for a new state park to be called Allegheny Gorge. The tract included some 10 kilometers (6 miles) along the Allegheny River where it has cut a canyon more than 150 meters (500 feet) deep through the plateau. The land had been heavily used in the past, first for subsistence farming, then for charcoal iron manufacturing, and, more recently, for gas and oil drilling. Funds to develop the new park did not materialize, and the land became part of Clear Creek State Forest. With an adjoining tract of State Game Land No. 39, the area is more than 1,600 hectares (3,950 acres). Cooperation between the Bureau of Forestry and the Grove City College Outing Club produced a network of hiking trails and cross-country ski trails above and along the Allegheny River, and an impressive overlook has been cleared.

Allegheny Gorge is most easily reached from new PA 8. Exit at PA 308, and turn northwest toward Pearl. Turn right on old PA 8 for 0.4 mile, and then turn right on Dennison Run Road (T-368). Continue east for 1.7 miles, and then turn right on Dewoody Road (T-371) for 1.2 miles to a game commission parking lot at the end of the road. Either hiking boots or good walking shoes should work for this hike.

To start, head south from the parking lot along the gated game commission management road. Allegheny Gorge is well supplied with trail signs, and virtually every junction is signed. At 0.4 km (0.2 mile) bear left on an old road that leads into the woods.

Old iron furnace along Bullion Run

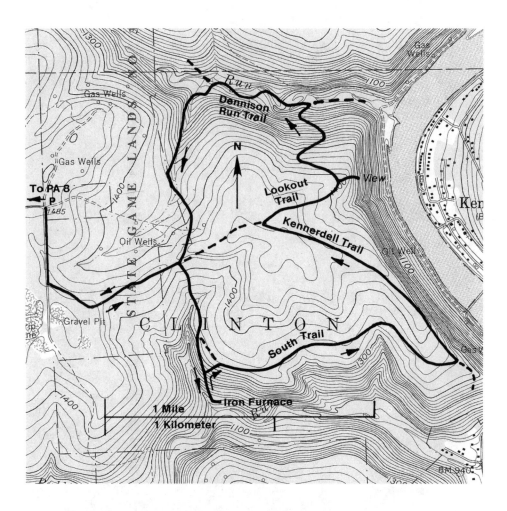

All the trails are marked with orange blazes, and in addition there are chartreuse blobs that may be useful. Old earthworks are encountered at 1.2 km (0.7 mile). They are thought to be bog iron pits, which provided iron ore for several local furnaces. The pits can be followed for long distances at this elevation since they followed the outcrop of ore.

Cross the boundary of state forest land at 1.4 km (0.9 mile). Soon you turn right for Bullion Run Iron Furnace at the major trail junction. You will return on one of the other blazed trails at this junction.

Cross a new logging road, and continue past a spring to the right of the trail. Then cross a bridge over a small stream in a hemlock forest. Bear right at 1.9 km (1.2 miles) for the iron furnace. The trail follows an old road down a tributary of Bullion Run. Unlike other parts of the state, here charcoal was made at the furnace rather than out in the woods. This road was used to bring the necessary iron ore and wood. Apparently the lure of hauling wood to the furnace was too much for the farmers, and subsistence farming collapsed in favor of a cash economy.

When you reach the bottom, turn left

above Bullion Run Iron Furnace. A view of the stack has been cleared, and a sign provides information on the operation of the furnace, which was built in 1840 and operated for only 10 years. Only eight or nine men were employed in its operation. It consumed 100 acres of woodland per year for charcoal but shut down over the summer. It could produce 3 tons of pig iron per day, which was hauled to the Allegheny River for shipment to Pittsburgh aboard white-pine rafts that floated down from Tionesta every spring.

After you've seen the furnace, climb back up the trail through the hemlock grove, and bear right at 2.9 km (1.8 miles) on a trail to Kennerdell. Bear right again at the trail junction at the top of the hill. This trail takes you through open woods at the edge of the plateau above Bullion Run and shows signs of mountain bikers practicing their extreme sport in this remote location. Little evidence remains of the oil wells near the junction with Kennerdell Road.

At 5.0 km (3.1 miles) turn left on the Kennerdell Road. The trail sign here identifies it only as a cross-country ski trail, and it's obscure until you reach the edge of the gorge. Orange-blazed like all the other trails, it goes along the edge of the plateau above the Allegheny River. Note an oil pipeline of small diameter that soon crosses the road and then parallels it. Turn right at 6.5 km (4.1 miles) on the Lookout Trail to reach Dennison Point Overlook.

The overlook is a good 120 meters (400 feet) above the Allegheny. Part of the village of Kennerdell can be seen across the river,

and you can also see far up river.

At this point you could truncate the hike by retracing your steps and turning right on the Kennerdell Trail, but a great deal of time and money has been expended in building four suspension bridges across Dennison Run, so you may as well take advantage of them.

Just behind the overlook, turn right on the orange-blazed Dennison Run Trail, and follow it carefully down an eroded old road to the stream. The trail is a bit obscure near the top of the hill. At 8.2 km (5.1 miles) turn left upstream, and cross the first of the suspension bridges. Continue upstream across two more suspension bridges to a trail junction at 8.9 km (5.5 miles).

Turn left at a sign for Bullion Run Iron Furnace, and cross the fourth suspension bridge. Continue upstream, crossing a bridge over a side stream. Then turn left and climb steeply, passing cascades and small waterfalls. Near the top, cross a bridge over the stream, and continue past an old oil or gas well.

Turn right on a woods road at 10.0 km (6.2 miles) and then bear left on trail. In just 200 more meters (650 feet) you reach the major trail junction with the Iron Furnace and Kennerdell Trails. Bear right and retrace your steps to the game lands parking lot and your car.

There are additional hiking opportunities here in the Allegheny River Tract. The Pipeline and Ridge Trails make a loop to the north of Dennison Run. Access to these trails is provided by two parking lots along T-368. The state forest map will suggest other loops.

50

M. K. Goddard State Park

Distance: 20.6 km (12.8 miles)

Time: 6 hours

Rise: 165 meters (540 feet)

Highlight: Lake Wilhelm

Maps: USGS 7½' Sandy Lake, New Lebanon, Hadley; state park map

Maurice K. Goddard State Park, around Lake Wilhelm in Mercer County, honors a Penn State forestry professor who became head of the Pennsylvania Department of Forests and Waters in 1955. Dr. Goddard served in the cabinets of more governors than anyone else in the history of the state. When the Department of Environmental Resources was created in 1971, he became secretary and served until 1979. One ambition of Dr. Goddard's was to have a state park within 40 kilometers (25 miles) of every citizen in the commonwealth. Lake Wilhelm is a flood-control reservoir named for Lawrence J. Wilhelm, director of the Mercer County Soil and Water Conservation District and a Mercer County commissioner.

This long hike is a real boot buster, but a great deal of effort has been expended on these trails, and the footway is excellent. Even the tiniest streams pass through culverts so there are scarcely any wet spots. There is only one real climb, but there's a lot of gentle up-and-down walking. By spotting a car in the parking lot below the dam, the hike could be turned into two 10-km (6.2-mile) car shuttle hikes.

The trailhead can be reached from exit 130 on I-79. Turn west on PA 358 for 0.4 mile, and then bear right on SR 1011. After 1.1 miles turn right on SR 1009, and proceed north for 2.3 miles, passing under I-79 and over Lake Wilhelm. Then turn left into boat launch no. 3, and park there. (If you want to get a park map, the office is just 0.1 mile farther up the concrete road.)

Despite the length of this hike, you might

get away with good walking shoes due to the generally good footway, but hiking boots are preferable. Despite the absence of blazing and a shortage of trail signs, the way is usually easy to follow except when crossing fields and some other open areas. Where it crosses roads, the path is usually obstructed with a single post bearing five or six yellow stripes at a 45 degree angle. Although these posts are not intended to mark the trail, they're frequently useful in spotting where it exits at the far side of an open area or where it jogs across a road.

To start the hike, head back up the entrance road and cross the concrete highway with care. Positive posting decals show that the trail is closed to horses but not bikes. Pass a large sign marking the start of the Lake Wilhelm Trail, and follow the mowed path through alternating meadows and patches of woods. In the fall the meadows are filled with goldenrod. Note the bluebird houses at many points along the trail. If these houses are serviced daily to expel starlings and house sparrows during the spring, there should be a bumper crop of bluebirds.

Soon the trail passes through a couple of old stone walls. Many of the meadows are reverting to woods. Note the prevalence of small crab apples coming up among the goldenrod. From the meadows there are frequent views of Lake Wilhelm, which fills the long narrow valley of Sandy Creek.

At 1.7 km (1.1 miles) pass a large maple tree that must have grown here when these woods were still fields. Note that the bridges on this trail have been built to accommodate the snowmobiles that use this trail in winter.

Cross a paved road at 2.2 km (1.4 miles) that leads right to boat launch no. 4. In season there are rest rooms and drinking water at all the boat launches and the Goddard Marina. The Lake Wilhelm Trail continues through alternating woods and meadows.

At 3.2 km (2.0 miles) you reach the first challenge to your pathfinding skill in the shape of a big meadow with no mowed swath. Turn right, proceed along the lakeshore, and then bear left to a bridge over the next stream. At 3.6 km (2.2 miles) you reach another large field. Turn sharply right along the edge of this field, and continue along the lake edge and around a small patch of woods. On the far side you pick up the mowed swath where it passes through a line of trees.

Soon the trail emerges at the edge of yet another field. Continue along this same line of trees into the next field, and follow it to the far corner. Here there is a snowmobile bridge over a stream.

At 4.8 km (3.0 miles) jog right 20 meters (65 feet) on an old road, and then go through a clearing, passing a low structure of concrete and steel. Continue as before through alternating woods and meadows. At one point the trail comes very close to the lake, and there's an old stone wall on the left.

At 7.3 km (4.5 miles) turn left on a gravel road and then right on the paved Lake Road. (This is the eastern limit of the use of the Lake Wilhelm Trail by snowmobiles.) Keep on the paved road across Dugan Run, and turn right on trail at 7.6 km (4.7 miles).

Continue through more meadows and patches of woods. Soon the dam is visible ahead. At 9.8 km (6.1 miles) cross the spillway, and bear right along the top of the dam. Note that this is a flood control dam, so the water level is well below the spillway. Pass a stairway leading down the face of the dam to a parking lot and rest rooms. At 10.0 km (6.2 miles) cross Creek Road, which is paved at this point. Next comes the big climb of the day. At the top, keep right to a covered

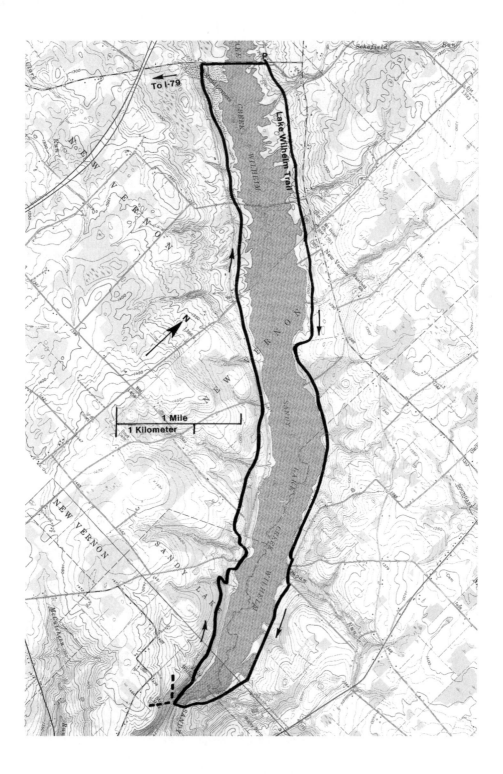

bench for the promised view of Lake Wilhelm. Alas, even with the leaves off you can't tell there's a lake down below—perhaps the permission to cut the small trees in the way never came through—but it does make a good stop for lunch. To continue, bear first right and then left to reach an old grade. The trail then switchbacks down the hill almost to the side of Creek Road.

At 10.6 km (6.6 miles) cross a pipeline swath and a bridge with concrete abutments. After proceeding along the edge of the hill for about 1.0 km (0.5 mile), the trail switchbacks down the side of the hill and crosses Creek Road at 11.9 km (7.4 miles).

Bear left through boat launch no. 1, and find the mowed trail at the far end of the parking lot. Recross Creek Road, and then cross Haun Road. Continue on in front of a garage. (The park map is in error at this point.)

Cross a stone bridge, and at 12.6 km (7.8 miles) turn left and climb through an old apple orchard. Turn right along the field edge at the top. A single blue diamond marks this trail for cross-country skiing.

At the far edge of the field, swing left above Irish Ridge Road. Then jog right on the gravel road for 30 meters (100 feet) and proceed along the edge of the woods. At 13.1 km (8.2 miles) enter the woods on a nice grade. These woods are unbroken and include an evergreen plantation.

Cross Creek Road for the last time at 14.6 km (9.0 miles) and continue in the narrow band of parkland between Lake Wilhelm and Creek Road. Cross a dirt road, and presently reach a parking area at 15.1 km (9.4 miles). This parking area, like the next, is not shown on the park map. There are occasional views of the lake, and you can see the fields on the far side that you traversed earlier in the day.

At 16.0 km (10.0 miles) you jog left at another evergreen plantation and go through a picnic area to reach the water pump in boat launch no. 2. Go diagonally left across the parking lot, and pick up the trail at the far corner. Continue through the woods. Note how all the streams are crossed on culverts. Pass through a parking area at 17.5 km (10.9 miles). A big maple is passed at 18.1 km (11.2 miles) and a big oak now almost dead at 18.9 km (11.7 miles).

At 19.0 km (11.8 miles) bear left on a paved road in the Goddard Marina, and follow it out to the concrete highway. Cross the highway, turn right facing traffic, and follow the causeway across Lake Wilhelm. Then turn left for boat launch no. 3.

Other hiking opportunities at M. K. Goddard State Park are the Falling Run Nature Trail, to the west near I-79, and the Goddard McKeever Trail, back at the dam.

Index

Let Backcountry Guides Take You There

Our experienced backcountry authors will lead you to the finest trails, parks, and back roads in the following areas:

50 Hikes Series
50 Hikes in the Maine Mountains
50 Hikes in Southern and Coastal Maine
50 Hikes in Vermont
50 Hikes in the White Mountains
50 More Hikes in New Hampshire
50 Hikes in Connecticut
50 Hikes in Massachusetts
50 Hikes in the Hudson Valley
50 Hikes in the Adirondacks
50 Hikes in Central New York
50 Hikes in Western New York
50 Hikes in New Jersey
50 Hikes in Eastern Pennsylvania
50 Hikes in Central Pennsylvania
50 Hikes in Western Pennsylvania
50 Hikes in the Mountains of North Carolina
50 Hikes in Northern Virginia
50 Hikes in Ohio
50 Hikes in Michigan

Walks and Rambles Series
Walks and Rambles on Cape Cod and the
    Islands
Walks and Rambles in Rhode Island
More Walks and Rambles in Rhode Island
Walks and Rambles on the Delmarva Peninsula
Walks and Rambles in Southwestern Ohio
Walks and Rambles in Ohio's Western Reserve
Walks and Rambles in the Western Hudson
    Valley
Walks and Rambles on Long Island
Walks and Rambles in and around St. Louis

25 Bicycle Tours Series
25 Bicycle Tours in Maine
25 Bicycle Tours in Vermont
25 Bicycle Tours on Cape Cod and the Islands
30 Bicycle Tours in New Jersey
25 Bicycle Tours in the Adirondacks
30 Bicycle Tours in the Finger Lakes Region
25 Bicycle Tours in the Hudson Valley
25 Bicycle Tours in the Twin Cities and
    Southeastern Minnesota
30 Bicycle Tours in Wisconsin
25 Bicycle Tours in Ohio's Western Reserve
25 Bicycle Tours in Maryland
25 Bicycle Tours on Delmarva
25 Bicycle Tours in and around
    Washington, D.C.
25 Bicycle Tours in Coastal Georgia and the
    Carolina Low Country
25 Bicycle Tours in the Texas Hill Country
    and West Texas
The Mountain Biker's Guide to Ski Resorts
25 Mountain Bike Tours in Vermont
25 Mountain Bike Tours in Massachusetts
25 Mountain Bike Tours in the Adirondacks
25 Mountain Bike Tours in the Hudson Valley
25 Mountain Bike Tours in New Jersey

Backroad Bicycling in Connecticut
Bicycling America's National Parks: California
Bicycling America's National Parks: Utah &
    Colorado

We offer many more books on hiking, fly-fishing, travel, nature, and other subjects. Our books are available at bookstores and outdoor stores everywhere. For more information or a free catalog, please call 1-800-245-4151 or write to us at The Countryman Press, P.O. Box 748, Woodstock, Vermont 05091. You can find us on the Internet at www.countrymanpress.com.